Matilda Ormond Taylor Birchard Abbey

Genealogy of the family of Lt. Thomas Tracy, of Norwich, Connecticut

Matilda Ormond Taylor Birchard Abbey

Genealogy of the family of Lt. Thomas Tracy, of Norwich, Connecticut

ISBN/EAN: 9783337723804

Printed in Europe, USA, Canada, Australia, Japan

Cover: Foto ©ninafisch / pixelio.de

More available books at **www.hansebooks.com**

LT. THOMAS TRACY,

OF NORWICH, CONNECTICUT.

COMPILED FROM THE GENEALOGICAL WORKS OF THE HYDES AND TRACY'S BY CHANCELLOR REUBEN H. WALWORTH AND OTHER RELIABLE SOURCES.

BY MRS. MATILDA O. ABBEY,

MILWAUKEE, WISCONSIN.

MILWAUKEE:
D. S. HARKNESS & CO., PRINTERS.
1889.

1243876

Tracy

Memoria Pie Æterna

THE TRACY'S

The following, compiled from the celebrated works of the Hyde's and Tracy's, by Chancellor Reuben H. Walworth, proves that Lieut. Thomas Tracy, of Norwich, Conn., was a direct descendant of the Saxon Kings, of England.

The Princess Gode, youngest daughter of King Ethelred II, his last wife was Emma, of Normandy, daughter of Richard I, Duke of Normandy, held lands in Gloucestershire in the reign of her brother, King Edward the Confessor, (see 2, Ellis' Doomsday book, 119), which lands remain in the hands of her descendants at this time. She married for her first husband, Dreux, Count of Vexin, called by English historians, Walter de Mante, Count of Mantes. He was great grand-son of Waleran who succeeded Hugh, the great Duke of France, father of Hugh Capet, as count of Vexin, in 956, and is said to be descended from Emperor Charlemagne and Hildegarde of Swabia, his wife. He went on a pilgrimage to Jerusalem, and died in Bythinia, about the first of July, 1035, and she died in 1054. They had four sons: first, Gauther, same name as Walter; second, Rudolph or Ralph; third, Toulgues; fourth, Pontoise.

General Rudolph or Ralph de Mantes, their second son was Lord of the Manor of Sudeley and of Toddington, which he inherited from his mother. He was created Earl of Hereford by his uncle, Edward the Confessor, of which earldom his son was deprived in the reign of William the Conqueror. He married Gethe, who held lands in her own right in Buckinghamshire, and who, in Doomsday book, is called Gethe, wife of Earl Rudolph.

He died the 21st of Dec., 1057, and was buried at Petersborough.

Harold de Mantes, their only son, married Matilda, daughter of Hugh Lupus, the first Earl of Chester, and Ermitrude his wife, and had by her two sons, John de Sudeley and Robert de Ewas.

John, the eldest son, inherited the lands of his father, in Gloucestershire, and became John de Sudeley, Lord of Sudeley and Toddington. He married Grace Tracy, daughter and heiress of Henry de Tracy, Feudal Lord of Barnstable, in Devonshire. They had two sons, Ralph the heir of the father, and William de Sudeley, who inherited the lands of his mother, and assumed her family name of Tracy.

Sir William Tracy, the second son, knight of Gloucestershire held lands at Toddington to the extent of one knights fee, from his brother Ralph de Sudely. He was one of the knights who, at the command of Henry II, assassinated Thomas A. Becket. He died in Devonshire and was burried in the church of Marthoe, (see Fuller's church history, Polwheles history of Devonshire.)

Sir Oliver Tracy, his eldest son and heir, was one of the knights of Gloucestershire in the time of King John, and as early as 1695 he was in possession of the estates of Barnstable.

William Tracy, his son, of Toddington, was in arms against King John in 1215, and his property was confiscated, but it was restored to him by Henry III, about 1217. He married Hawis de Born, and died about 1224.

Henry Tracy, his son and heir, of Toddington, died about 1246, and had two sons and one daughter.

Henry Tracy, of Toddington, his eldest son and heir, was presented to the church of Marthoe, in Devonshire, in 1275.

Sir William Tracy, of Toddington, his son and heir, was one of the knights of Gloucestershire in 1290, and had a command in the Scottish war.

His son, William Tracy of Toddington, was a ward of Lawrence Tresham in 1300. He was one of the knights of Gloucestershire, and was sheriff for five years, commencing in 1324. In

1313 he was elected to Parliament as one of the knights of Gloucestershire, and again in 1321. (The office of sheriff in those days was a situation of great dignity and importance, very different from now.)

William Tracy, of Toddington, his son and heir, had a mandate to raise troops for the King, in the seventh Edward III, from the county of Gloucestershire.

Sir John Tracy, of Toddington, his son and heir, was in Parliament as one of the knights of Gloucestershire in 1357, and was sheriff in 1368-1269.

Sir John Tracy, his eldest son, of Toddington, was a member of Parliament, he was sheriff of Gloucestershire in 1378, and died in 1379.

William Tracy, of Toddington, his son and heir, was sheriff of Gloucestershire in 1395, and died in 1399.

William Tracy, of Toddington, his son and heir, was sheriff of Gloucestershire in 1418, and in 1431 was called to the privy council of King Henry VI. He married Alice, the widow of William Gifford, and daughter and heiress of Guy de la Spine, Lord of the manor of Coughton, in Warwickshire.

William Tracy, of Toddington, their eldest son and heir, was sheriff of Gloucestershire in 1443-1444-1450. He married Margaret Pauncefort, daughter of Sir John Pauncefort and Margaret Beauchamp, his first wife.

Henry Tracy, Esq., of Toddington, their eldest son and heir, married Alice Baldington, daughter and co-heiress of Thomas Baldington, Esq., of Alderly, and died about 1506.

Sir William Tracy, of Toddington, their eldest son and heir, was sheriff of Gloucestershire in 1513. He married Margaret Trockmorton, daughter of Sir Thomas Trockmorton of Ass Court, and Margaret Ordney, his wife, and grand-daughter of Sir John Trockmorton, who married Eleanor, daughter and co-heiress of Sir Guy de la Spine, Lord of the manor of Coughton in Warwickshire, and died about 1531. He was one of the first who embraced the reformed religion, in the time of King Henry VIII.

In his will, instead of leaving his soul to God through the intercession of the Virgin Mary and the rest of the Saints, according to the then common form, he stated briefly his belief as a Christian, and his hope of salvation by the grace and merit of the Saviour, and then proceeds as follows: "As touching the wealth of my soul, the faith that I have taken and rehearsed is sufficient as I suppose without any other man's works or merits. My ground and belief is that there is but one God and one mediator between God and man, which is Jesus Christ. So that I accept none other in heaven or earth to mediate between me and God, all others to be but petitioners in receiving grace, and therefore will I bestow no part of my goods for the intent that any man shall say or do ought to help my soul. For therein I trust only to the promises of Christ. He that believeth and is baptised shall be saved, and he who believes not shall be damned." This will was condemned as heretical, and the testator's body was raised and burned in 1532. He left two sons: first, William, who was ancestor of the Viscounts Tracy, of Rathcoole, in the peerage of Ireland, and of Robert Tracy, who was one of the English judges from 1700 to 1726; second, Richard Tracy.

Richard Tracy, Esq., of Stanway, the second son, was sheriff of Gloucestershire in 1559. He obtained grants of lands from the Crown at Stanway and at Beckford, in the county which had belonged to the suppressed Abbey of Tewksbury, (see first Plow., Rep. 7145.) He was a man of good education, and prior to the death of Edward VI. wrote several treaties in defence of his fathers' faith, the most remarkable of which was entitled "Preparations for the Cross," written in 1550. He married Barbara Lucy, pupil of Fox, the Martyrologist, she was daughter of Thomas Lucy, of Charlecote, in Warwickshire, and it was her nephew on whom Shakespeare took revenge, by writing in one of his plays as Justice Shallow, as it was before Sir Thomas Lucy, Shakespeare was arraigned for deer stealing. Richard Tracy, Esq., of Stanway, and Barbara Lucy had three sons and three daughters. He was sheriff of Gloucestershire in 1560, Barbara

Lucy, his wife, was a descendant in the sixteenth generation from Hugh de Mountfort, son of Gilbert de Gamet and Alice Mountfort, and great grand-son of Baldwin V. Count of Flanders, who married Alice, daughter of Robert II, King of France. Through her ancestress, Judith, wife of Baldwin, the first Count of Flanders, Barbara Lucy was descended from the Emperor Charlemagne, and through his ancestors, Alfritha, wife of Baldwin II, Count of Flanders, she was descended from Alfred the Great, and other Saxon kings of England.

Nathaniel Tracy, of Tewksbury, their second son received lands from his father at that place.

Lieut. Thomas Tracy, son of Nathaniel Tracy, came from Tewksbury, where he was born, in 1610, to New England. He landed at Salem, where he stayed until Feb. 23, 1637. He came over in the interest of his friends, Lord Say and Lord Brooks. He soon left the bay for the old colony on the Connecticut river in 1640, and there married the widow Mason in 1641, at Wethersfield, afterward moved to Saybrook, named after his friends. 'Tis an old, substantial, euphonious name, interesting from its historical associations. Lord Say and Lord Brook with their associates were the patentees of Connecticut. Their patent was received from Robert, Earl of Warwick, in 1632, and extended along the New England coast, westward from the Narragansett river 120 miles, and in latitude and breadth to the South Sea. The Earl of Warwick was president of the Council of Plymouth, incorporated by King James the First, for the settlement of New England, and authorized to dispense grants and patents to others. The patents were therefore valid and clear. The place of immediate importance in this patent, was the point at the mouth of the Connecticut river. And here John Winthrop acting under commission from the patentees, built a fort and commenced a plantation in 1625 to 1636. The Pequot war followed soon after the establishment, and threatened the annihilation of the infant settlement. The fort was frequently surrounded by bloodthirsty savages.

Thomas Tracy had by his first wife, the widow Mason, seven children: first, John, born 1642; second, Thomas, about 1644; third, Jonathan, 1646; fourth, Miriam, about 1648; fifth, Solomon, 1651; sixth, Daniel, 1651; seventh, Samuel, 1654, who died in 1693, unmarried. The first two children were born in Netherstield, the others in Saybrook, where he lived many years before removing to Norwich, Conn., where he was one of the proprietors of the nine mile grant.

John. Lieut. Thomas Tracy's first son, married Mary Winslow, June 10, 1670, resided in Duxbury, Mass. The bride was a daughter of Josiah Winslow, the elder, who was a brother to Gov. Edward Winslow, of Plymouth. It is a mistake about her being the daughter of John Winslow and his wife, of the Mayflower. (From Mrs. Calkin's celebrated book on Norwich.)

Thomas Tracy, second son, born 1642. The name of his wife is not recorded. He had eight children: Nathaniel, Sarah, Jeremiah, Daniel, Thomas, Jediah, Deborah and Jerusha. His will was dated April 6, 1721, but not proved until 1724.

Jonathan Tracy, third son of Lieut. Thomas, was born in 1648, and married Mary Griswold, July 11, 1672. Their children were: Jonathan, Jr., Hannah, Christopher and Mary.

Miriam Tracy, only daughter, the fourth child of Lieut. Thomas Tracy, was born in 1649. Married Thomas Waterman, Nov. 1668. Their children were: Thomas, John, Elizabeth, Miriam, Martha, Lydia and Waterman. Thomas Waterman, her husband, was one of the original proprietors of Norwich.

Thomas Waterman, her eldest son, married Elizabeth Allyn, and John, her second son, first married Elizabeth Lathrop, second, Judith Woodward, third, Elizabeth Bassett. He was the father of William Waterman, who married Margaret Tracy, and of Hannah Waterman, mother of Benedict Arnold, the traitor. Elizabeth Waterman, her eldest daughter, married Capt. John Fitch, of Windham, and had four children. Martha Waterman, her third daughter, married Deacon Reynold Marvin, of Lyme.

Dr. Solomon Tracy, fourth son of Lieut. Thomas, was born

1651. He first married Sarah Huntington, Nov. 23, 1676; second Sarah Bliss, widow of Thomas Sherman, April 8, 1686. Their children by the first wife were Lydia and Simon, and by second wife, Solomon Tracy. Simon died July 9, 1782.

Daniel Tracy, fifth son, born 1652, married Abigail Adgate, Sept. 9, 1682, second wife, Hannah Bingham, widow of Thomas Bingham, March 4, 1711. Their children by the first wife were Daniel and Abigail; by the second wife, Elizabeth and Samuel. Daniel Tracy, Sen., died July 29, 1728.

Samuel Tracy, sixth son, died June 11, 1693, without issue.

The youngest son of Thomas Tracy, who was the son of Lieut. Thomas Tracy, was Jedediah Tracy, of Preston, who died June 8, 1779. His father, Thomas Tracy, son of Lieutenant, died April 6, 1721.

Deacon Jedediah died at the age of 87 years. His death was caused by being thrown from a horse, (gay old fellow to be riding at that age) he had been deacon of his church fifty years. He was Magistrate and Representative of the town. He left one hundred and thirty-seven direct descendents. Good for you Jedediah.

Lieut. Thomas Tracy was evidently a man of talent and activity, skillful in the management of various kinds of business. He took great interest in ship-building, and did not think it a degradation to use his hands as well as his mind. The confidence placed in him by his associates is manifested in the great number of appointments which he received. His name is on the roll of the Legislature as representative of Norwich, at twenty-seven sessions. The elections were semi-annual, and Mr. Tracy was chosen twenty-one times, beginning October 9, 1662, and ending July 5, 1684. The others were extra sessions. In August 1673, he was lieutenant of the "New London County Dragoons," enlisting to fight the Dutch and Indians.

These six John Tracy's were in the line of primogeniture, and natives of Norwich, except the first one.

John Tracy, the second son, was born in 1673. He married

Elizabeth Leffingwell, daughter of Thomas Leffingwell, the 2d, of Norwich. He was born Aug. 27, 1649. The eldest son Lieut. Thomas Leffingwell, was one of the original proprietors of Norwich. He was born at Croix Hall, England, and was one of the first settlers of Saybrook.

Thomas Leffingwell, the second son, came to Norwich in 1660, being then 11 years old. He married Mary Bushnell, who was born Jan. 8, 1655, at Saybrook. The eldest daughter of Richard Bushnell and Mary Marvin, of Saybrook.

John Tracy, third son, born 1702, married Margaret Hyde.

John Tracy, fourth son, was born at Norwich, Conn., Feb. 11, 1725, was the eldest son of John Tracy and Margaret Hyde, of Norwich. He married Oct. 13, 1747, his third cousin, Margaret Huntington, born Nov. 23, 1724, at Norwich, daughter of Christopher Huntington and Abigail Alel-Lathrop. His children by her were: John 5th, born at Norwich, married Lester Dridge; Mary, born April, 1750, at Norwich, married Andrew Hyde; Margaret, born May 29, 1753, at Norwich, married first, Zebediah Lathrop, second Benjamin Stoors; Lydia, born 1775, died unmarried.

John Tracy, born at Norwich, Conn., Dec. 21, 1755, eldest son of John Tracy and Margaret Huntington. He married May 24, 1780, Esther Pride, of Lisbon. In 1806 they removed to Columbus, N. Y., where he died June 14, 1821.

His first son John, was born Oct. 26, 1783, at Norwich, married Susannah Hyde. He was a lawyer, and they settled at Oxford. He was Lieutenant Governor of the state for six years. They were living at Oxford in 1852. They had three children, born at Oxford. The first, John, born June 29, 1820. He was the seventh John in descent from Lieut. Thomas Tracy. This John died Dec. 24, 1820, living only a few months.

Lieut. Joshua Tracy, born at Norwich, Conn., Aug. 13, 1745. The seventh son of John Tracy and Margaret Hyde, of Norwich, was grand-son of John Hyde, of the third generation. He married, May 2 1771, Naoma Bingham, of Windham, born May

13, 1744, daughter of Jonathan Bingham and Mary Abbey, of Windham, grand-daughter of John Abbey, the first, of Windham, Mass. He died March, 1777, at Norwich, Conn., of smallpox, and was burried on the hill at Franklin, near Dr. Woodwards. Their children were: Abel, born April 26, 1772, at Norwich; Thomas, born May 23, 1774, at Norwich, was educated at Yale, and died at Baltimore, unmarried; Joshua, born Dec. 21, 1776, at Norwich, died Aug. 11, 1779.

Abel Tracy, son of Lieut. Joshua, was the grand-father of the celebrated artist, Mr. John Martin Tracy. His home for a few years has been Greenwich, Conn., where he moved from New York, as his specialty is cattle painting, for which he is famous. He left the Sophomore Class of the Northwestern University, of Evanston, Ill., to enlist in the army; he served through the war, reaching the grade of Lieutenant. After ths war he went on a tour of the Eastern States, and forming the acquaintance of several artists, he decided to adopt the profession of painting. He went at once to Paris, and soon entered the Ecole dis Beaux arts, and atelier of Isidor Pils, intending to become a painter of battles. After the death of his master, he went for some years under the instruction of Caroleas Daran, and he began an accidental but most encouraging career as a portrait painter. During the Franco-Prussian war, he was in America, and traveled for two years in California and the far west generally, returning to Paris in 1874. He married Melamia, daughter of August Guillman, the celebrated pastel portrait painter. His wife's family, on the father's side, have all been professional artists since a time when there is no record to the contrary. The brother of his wife, Emile Guillman, is to-day one of the most eminent of those sculptors who devote themselves to bronzes. Her mother is of the family of Chamfflewey, the novelist and writer on Ceramics, etc.

DEED OF NORWICH.

Know all men that Onkos, Owaneco, Attawanhood, Sachems of Mohegan have Bargained, sold and passed over, and doe by these Presents sell and pass over unto the Towne and Inhabitants of Norwich nine miles squar of land lying and being at the Mohengen and the parts thereunto ajoyneing, with all ponds, rivers, woods, quarries, mines, with all royalties, privileges, and appurtenances thereunto belonging, to them the said inhabitants to Norwich, theire heirs and successors forever—the said lands are to be bounded as followeth, viz: to the southward on the west side of the Great River, ye line to be begin at the brooke falling into the head of Trading Cove, and soe to run west norwest seven miles—from thence the line to run nor northeast nine miles, and on the East side the afores'd river to the southward the line is to joyne with New London bounds as it is now laid out and soe to run east two miles from the foresd river, and soe from thence the line is to run nor noreast nine miles and from thence to run nor norwest nine miles to meet with the western line.——In consideration whereof the sd Onkos, Owaneco and Attawanhood doe acknowledge to have received of the parties aforesd the full and juste sum of one hundred and seventy pounds and doe promise and engage ourselves, heirs and successors, to warrant the sd bargain and sale to the aforesd parties, their heirs and successors and them to defend from all claims and molestations from any whatsoever.— In witness whereof we have hereunto set to our hands this 6th of June, Anno 1659.

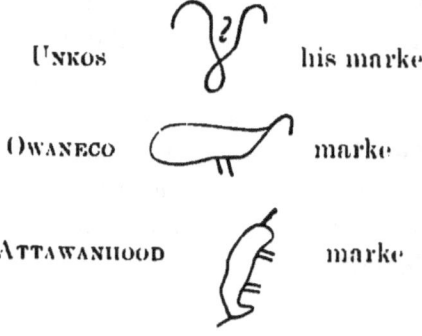

Unkos   his marke

Owaneco   marke

Attawanhood   marke

Witness hereunto
    John Mason
    Thomas Tracy

This deed is recorded in the County Booke Agust 20, 1663: as atests   JOHN ALLYN, Sec'y.

The bounds of this tract, as more particularly described in the first volume of the Proprietors' Records, were as follows:

The line commenced at the mouth of Trading Cove, where the brook falls into the cove; thence W. N. W. seven miles to a Great Pond, (now in the corner of Bozrah and Colchester,) the limit in this direction being denoted by a black oak marked N, that stood near the outlet of the "Great Brook that runs out of the pond to Norwich river;" thence N. N. E. nine miles to a black oak standing on the south side of the river (Shetucket) "a little above Waw-mi-ag-wang;" thence S. S. E. nine miles, crossing the Shetucket and the Quinebaug, and passing through "a Seader Swamp called Catantaquak," to a white oak tree marked N, thirteen rods beyond a brook called Quo-qui-qua-song, the space from the Quinebaug to this tree being just one mile and fifty-eight rods; thence S. S. W. nine miles to a white oak marked N, near the dwelling-houses of Robert Allyn and Thomas Rose, where Norwich and New London bounds join; thence west on the New London bounds, crossing the southern part of Mr. Brewster's land, two miles to Mohegan river, opposite the mouth of Trading Cove brook, where the first bounds began.

Such were the bounds, as reviewed and renewed in October, 1685, by an authorized committee, accompanied by two sachems and some of the chief men of Mohegan. The former deed of 1659, with the boundaries thus described and explained, was then ratified and confirmed by "Owaneco, sachem of Mohegan, son and heire unto Owaneco," in a new deed, signed by them Oct. 5, 1685, witnessed by John Arnold and Stephen Gifford, and acknowledged before James Fitch, Assistant.

The southern boundary line, it will be observed, is nine miles in length, two east of the river, and seven west, without counting the breadth of the Thames, and the length of Trading Cove to the mouth of the brook, which would make this line nearly ten miles long. This is explained in the deed to be designed as a compensation for "the benefit and liberty of the waters and river for fishing and other occasions," reserved to the Indians.

FIRST HOUSE LOTS, 1660.

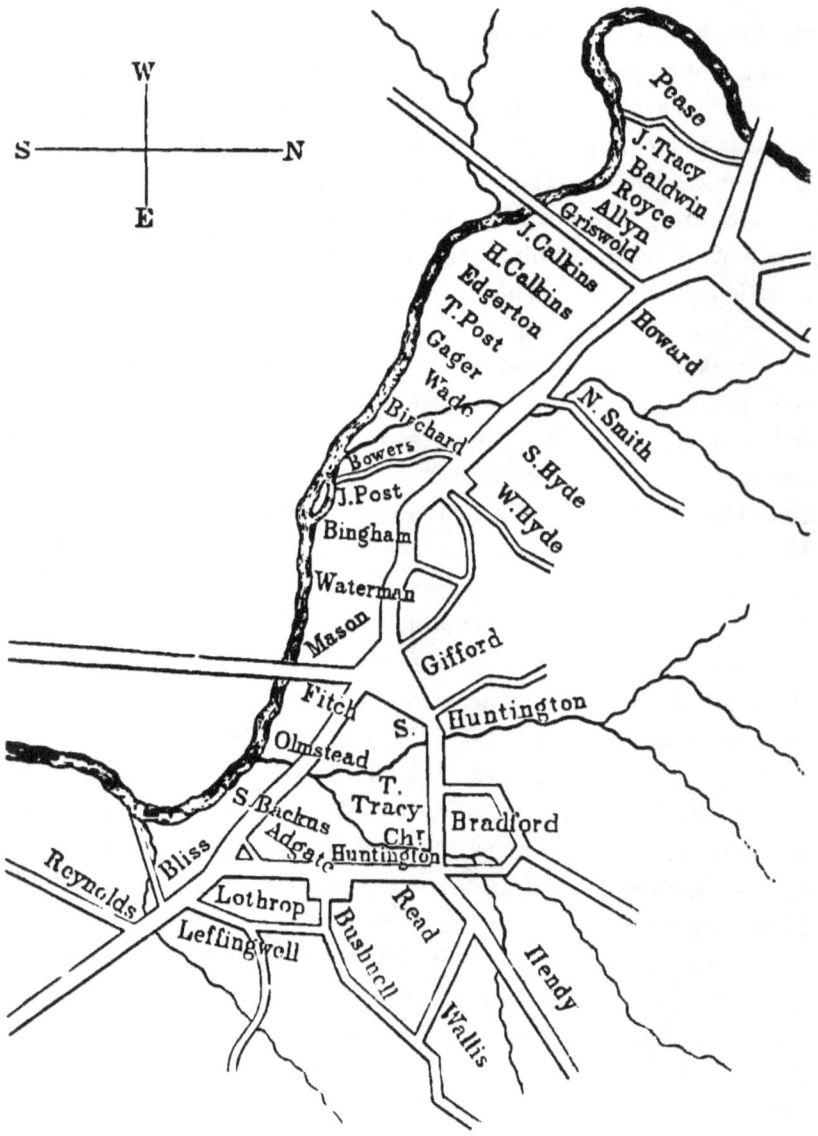

Extract from a half century sermon delivered in the First Society of Lisbon, Dec. 5, 1854, by the Rev. Levi Nelson, pastor of the First Congregational Church in that place.

The Tracy family, Lieut. Thomas Tracy, came from England, arrived at Salem. Mass., where he staid for a short time, removed to Saybrook, Conn., then to Norwich. His son Thomas settled in that part of Norwich which is now near Preston. Thomas Jr's. son Jeremiah, became a land holder in Newent, bordering on the Quinebaug river. He was one of the first settlers, and joined the church when it was organized in 1723. He was the father of Deacon Andrew Tracy.

Andrew Tracy, of Lisbon, Conn., was born Feb. 16, 1722, married Ruth Smith, daughter of Capt. Elija Smith, of Barnstable, Mass. She was born July 18, 1725. His first son was Ebenezer Tracy, born April 20, 1744. He first married Mary Freeman; second, Thankful Ayres; third, Anna Berry. Their children were: Eliza, Ziporah, Mary, Sarah, Lydia, the last was the mother of Mr. Henry Allen, of Norwich, Conn., Rebecca, Ebenezer, Jr. and Frederick, who died the same day he was born.

Jesse Tracy was born Dec. 20, 1745, married Faith Bingham. Their children were: Lucy, Jesse, Jr., Freeman, Hannah, Jedediah, Andrew, Erastus, Anna and Felix.

Sarah Tracy married Jedediah Lathrop, had ten children. The names and ages are on the City Records,

Andrew Tracy, Jr., married Anna Bingham, of Windham, Sept. 17, 1771. He died Dec. 28,1819, aged 69 years. His wife Anna, died Sept. 8, 1827, aged 77 years. They had eight children: Lemuel Tracy, born July 29, 1763, died April 6, 1865, aged 82; Ruth Tracy, born March 30, 1775, died Oct. 17, 1856, aged 81; Lucy Tracy, born Nov. 4, 1777, died April 20, 1824, aged 47; Elias Tracy, born Jan. 22, 1780, died June 20, 1850, aged 70; Stephen Tracy, born July 2, 1782, died Oct. 23, 1836, aged 84; Anna Tracy, born Dec. 27, 1784, died March 1, 1829, aged 45; Andrew Tracy, Jr., born Jan. 25, 1789, died Jan. 8, 1861; Jesse

Tracy, born March 31, 1792, died March 30, 1857, aged 65 ; Elijah Tracy died at the age of 11 years.

Ruth Tracy married Israel Herrick, had seven children, and died at LeRoy, N. Y., aged 85. Mary Tracy married Nathan Taylor. They had eight children. Anna Tracy married Farwell Coit, had two children. The son, who did not marry, was Erastus Coit. The daughter married a Mr. Reynolds.

Mary Tracy, third daughter of Andrew Tracy, born Sept. 9, 1756, and Nathan Taylor, born Jan. 1752, were married April 24, 1783. Their children were : Nathan, born May 25, 1785, died Jan. 1, 1865 ; Mary, born April 26, 1787, died May 8, 1872 ; Tracy, (twin to Mary) born April 26, 1787, died Feb. 23, 1832 ; John, born Dec. 20, 1789, died June 20, 1877 ; George, born January 5, 1793, died August, 1834 ; William, born March 18, 1795, died June 8, 1881 ; Lydia, born Oct. 6, 1797, died Sept. 18, 1885 ; Elias, born Jan. 5, 1810, died aged about 30.

Jeremiah Tracy was born at Lisbon, Conn., Saturday, April 11, 1761, married Martha Lascelle, May 19, 1785 ; Martha Lascelle Tracy, born Monday, March 25, 1765 ; Olive Tracy, born July 4, 1786 ; Jeremiah, born April 21, 1788 ; Susannah, born Wednesday, June 9, 1790 ; Martha Tracy, born Monday, July 2, 1792 ; Jerusha Tracy, born Thursday, July 10, 1794, died Monday, May 2, 1796 ; Erastus Tracy, born April 12, 1797. Second Jerusha Tracy, born Monday, Aug. 17, 1799 ; Maria Tracy, born Tuesday, Nov. 17, 1801 ; Calvin Tracy, born Saturday, Nov. 5, 1803 ; Luther Tracy, born Feb. 11, 1805 ; Joshua Tracy, born 1807, cannot give the month.

Elizabeth Tracy married Grover Le Hommedian. He had two wives : by his first wife he had thirteen children, by Elizabeth, his second wife, six, in all nineteen children. Nothing small about his family.

David Tracy married Susannah Capron ; they had nine children. Mrs. Henry Allen, the wife of Mr. Henry Allen, of Norwich, Conn., and one of the oldest and most respected citizens, is the only one living of this large family. David died in Norwich, Conn.; George died while descending the Mississippi river; the Rev. William Tracy, a man of great purity and worth, went out to India, accompanied by his wife, who was in sympathy with him in his missionary labor. They and their children deeply lamented, now sleep in that far off land.

The descendants of Andrew Tracy are very numerous, and are to be found in many cities of the United States. Those of his daughter, Mary Tracy, who married Nathan Taylor, many are living in Philadelphia, Pa. Her son, Tracy Taylor,. was the first to leave his New England home; where his brothers George and William, soon followed him to Philadelphia. They were all interested in the iron business. In 1810 George and William established an importing house at 303 Branch street, making a specialty of tin plate. When they retired, their sons, Nathan and George conducted the business with the same integrity and energy that has always made the house of these honorable men so popular. Nathan and George are both dead; they were deeply lamented by relatives and friends. Mr. William Taylor has recently retired. The firm now is Mr. Nathan Taylor, Mr. Hollingshead and George Taylor, Jr. They now occupy stores 301-303-305 Branch street, Philadelphia. Mr. Nathan Taylor, of the present firm, married Miss Florence N. Supplee. Their children are Elizabeth H. Taylor, Florence O. Taylor and Natalie Taylor. Mr. Hollingshead W. Taylor married Miss Evaline Skillman; children are Aline Skillman Taylor and Hollingshead N. Taylor.

Tracy Taylor, grand-son of Andrew Tracy, was a man far above ordinary in intelligence and worth. He retired from the iron business, in which he was engaged for many years with his brothers George and William Taylor, in Philadelphia, and was an eminent jurist and a magistrate until his death in 1832. He married Miss Ann Henry, her father, John Henry, was a merchant in Philadelphia in the early days of that city. Her mother was Miss Knouse, sister to Jacob Knouse, a man highly respected. He left a large property that was distributed among his many descendants of Philadelphia and the Rising Sun, an adjoining place. The children of Ann and Tracy Taylor were:

Emily Ormond Taylor, married Mr. William Winberg, of Philadelphia, she died of consumption, childless; Albert Augustus, died young; Matilda Ormond Taylor married Harvey Birchard, of Milwaukee, who was an immediate descendant of John Birchard, one of the proprietors of Norwich, Conn. They have one son, Mr. Harvey L. Birchard, now twenty-eight years of age. Her second husband was Col. D. C. Abbey, now dead; Charles Hiram Taylor, second son of Ann and Tracy Taylor, was a physician graduate of the University of Pennsylvania, married Miss Mary Irick, daughter of Gen. Irick, of New Jersey. They had two children, Charles Tracy, and Mary, who died. Charles Tracy is a merchant in Philadelphia, married Miss Sophia Davis, grand-daughter of Mr. Cramp, the well known ship-builder of Philadelphia. Their children are Charles Keen Taylor, Harvey Birchard Taylor, Emily Cramp Taylor. Almira died unmarried; Alfred died, aged twenty-three, unmarried; DeWitt was a physician graduate at the Pennsylvania college, Philadelphia, and died of pneumonia; Tracy Watmough Taylor died in infancy.

Mr. William Taylor, brother to Tracy Taylor, married Miss Sarah Mollidor. Their only son, Nathan Taylor, was an energetic member of the firm of W. & G. Taylor, 803 Branch street, Philadelphia. He married Miss Charlot Cooper, of Philadelphia. Their sons were Nathan A. Taylor and Hollingshead Taylor.

George Taylor, brother to Nathan and Tracy Taylor, died in Philapelphia. He married Miss Augustine. Their children were: George E., married Miss Deal. George, his son, a member of the firm of N. and G. Taylor, of which his father was so long an honored and energetic member, is every way worthy of the high respect and confidence in which he is held. Maria, sister of George E., married Henry Elder; Cornelia married Granville Stokes; Julia is unmarried; William Y., married Miss McCullough, they have one daughter, Ella. Mr. John Taylor, brother to Tracy, George and Nathan Taylor, died in Philadelphia in 1876, unmarried.

Capt. Israel Hollister, born Dec. 16, married Mary Taylor,

twin-sister to Tracy Taylor, they were the children of Nathan and Mary Taylor, and grand-children of Andrew Tracy. Capt. Israel Hollister died May 12, 1853, aged 97, his wife, Mary, died May 8, 1872, aged 85. Their children were: Mary Maria Hollister, born June 5, 1815; Francis Israel, born July 30, 1817; Eliza Ann, born Feb. 20, 1820; Sarah, born, Nov. 22, 1823; William Tracy, born April 6, 1825. The Hollister's have always made their home in Connecticut. Mr. William T. Hollister and his esteemable wife, who was a Miss Abbey, lived at East Hartford. They have a son, Charles, and daughter, Miss Hattie Hollister. Erastus Coit, born July 31, 1827; Cornelia Matilda, born March 31, 1831, are dead.

Mr. Henry L. Palmer, of Milwaukee, president of the life insurance company, resides at 302 Juneau Avenue. He is the grand-son of Jeremiah Tracy, son of Andrew Tracy, of Lisbon, Conn. Mr. Palmer is one of the most respected men of the Northwest, and a high mason, being Puisant Sovereign Supreme Council, A. A., S. R., N. M., J., U. S. A.; Past Grand Master Knight Templer, U. S.; Past Grand Commander; Past High Priest: Past Grand Master Ancient Order of Scottish Rite, Jurisdiction of the United States of America. Mr. Palmer's family consists of a wife, children and sisters, all highly respected.

COPIED FROM THE MILWAUKEE TELEGRAPH OF FEB. 19, 1888.

Two or three times a day if you are watching, you will see a certain gentleman going from his handsome new residence on Juneau Avenue, to the New Insurance Building, on Broadway. His step never varies, his head bends a little to the right and he stoops slightly when he walks. He looks like a man who thinks a great deal, and who is capable of thinking deeply, and his looks in this respect do not belie him. Do you want to know something about this gentleman, Judge Henry Palmer. About forty years ago he came to Milwaukee a young lawyer, and this city has been his home ever since. He has been a Judge, a member of Assembly, a State Senator, a candidate for Governor, several times Grand Master of the Masons, Grand High Priest of the

Chapter, Grand Commander of the Knight Templer, head of the Wisconsin Consistory, and at the head of the 33° Masons, in the Northern Jurisdiction of North America. If I mistake not, he participated in the organization of all the grand masonic lodges in this state. There are men in Milwaukee upon whom he has conferred all of the degrees as masons, from entered apprentice, to the 33°. Without a doubt he has at his tongues end more of masonic ceremonies than any other living man. He takes an active part in conferring the degrees in the Wisconsin Consistory, every time there is a convocation. And the work of no man is more keenly appreciated by all the old membere and those who are receiving grades. He is a ready, able and pleasant public speaker, has the confidence and respect of all classes, and a very warm place in the affections of the masons every where in North America. Mr. Palmer is president of the North Western Mutual Life Insurance Company of Milwaukee.

Nathan Taylor, first son of Mary Tracy and Nathan Taylor, married Miss Sarah Hackstaff, Sept. 13, 1810. He died in Troy, N. Y., June 2, 1855. She was born Oct. 13, 1793, died in New York, June 1, 1862. They were both highly respected. Their children were: Charles Taylor, born Nov. 11, 1811, who was drowned: Herman Taylor, born Dec. 2, 1813, died at Peru, N. Y., Nov. 19, 1814; Tracy Taylor, born in New York, Feb. 15, 1819, died at Troy in 1857. He was Teller of the Troy bank for many years; Sarah Ann, born at Peru, N. Y., June 2, 1821, died Feb., 1887, in New York City; Mary I. Taylor married William Rhodes, July 7, 1849; George H. Taylor, born June 23, married Josephine Hicock. He was lost on the Ville du Havre. She left New York on Nov. 15, 1873, with more than three hundred souls aboard. She came in collission in mid-ocean with the ship Loch Earn, bound from London to New York. Within twelve minutes after the collission the Ville du Havre sank, carrying down two hundred and twenty-six men, women and children; eighty-seven were saved; Alfred Taylor is married and has two children, and lives at Orange, N. Y. Mr. Nathan Taylor was a man very much respected and was connected with large lumber interests.

ALLEN

THE SUDELEY'S.

From Burke's Peerage of 1886.

Sudeley, Baron, (Charles-Douglas-Richard-Hanbury-Tracy) of Toddington, county Gloucester, a lord in waiting to the Queen in 1880 to 1885, born July 3, 1840, married May 9, 1868, Ida-Maria-Catherine, daughter of the Hon. Frederick-James Tollamache, (brother of the Earl of Dysart) and has issue: first, Eva-Isabella-Henrietta, born Jan. 25, 1869; second, William-Charles, Frederick, born April 19, 1870; third, Algernon-Henry-Charles, born April 11, 1871; fourth, Florence-Emma-Louisa, born Feb. 11, 1873; fifth, Ida-Madeleine-Agnes, born Jan. 20, 1875; sixth, Alice-Evelyn-Agatha, born Aug. 12, 1877; seventh, Rhona-Margaret-Ida, born July 13, 1879; eighth, Felix-Charles-Hubert, born July 27, 1882. His lordship, who succeeded as fourth baron on the death of his brother, April 28, 1877, was formerly in the Royal Navy, which he entered in 1854, became lieutenant in 1860, and resigned his commission in 1863, having received medals for his services in the Baltic and China. He was subsequently called to the bar in January, 1866, and was M. P. for Montgomery from 1863 until his succession to the peerage.

The ancient family of Tracy boast of descent from Saxon Kings of England.

John de Sudeley, Lord of Sudeley and Toddington, A. D. 1140, married Grace, daughter and heir of Henry de Traci, feudal lord of Barnstable, and had issue. Ralph de Sudeley, founder of the priory of Erdburie; William, who adopted his mothers' name of De Traci.

The youngest son, William, assumed his mother's name of De Traci, lived in the reign of Henry II, and held lands of his brother Ralph de Sudley, by one knights fee, which was probably the manor of Toddington, for it appears by Doomesday book, that it was held by the Lord Sudeley, of the manor of Sudeley; and in the reign of Edward I, the Tracy's are expressly said to be possessed of it; and this William in a deed to Otwell, Lord of Sudeley, son and heir of the said Ralph, is called his uncle; this is, (almost beyond a doubt) the same Sir William Tracy, who was concerned in the assassination of Thomas A. Becket. Fuller, in his "Worthies," naming the assassin as Sir William Tracy, of Toddington, describes him as "a man of high birth, state and stomach, a favorite of the king's, and his daily attendants." In the 19th Henry II, he was created Steward of Normandy, which he held only two years; and he is again mentioned in 2 John. During the troublous reign of that monarch, William de Traci appeared in arms with the other barons, and had his lands confiscated; but they were restored to him by 2 Henry III, as is shown by a Roll, dated at Westwinster, Nov. 18, in that year. He also founded and endowed a chapel to Thomas A. Becket, in the conventual church at Tewksbury. He died aria, 1224. By Hawise de Born, his wife, (who married secondly, Hugh Fitzwilliam, Lord of Hatten, county Warwick) he left, with two daughters, the elder married to Sir Cervase Courtenay, and the younger to William de Arden; a son and successor.

Henry de Tracy, of Toddington, county Gloucester, who died about the year 1246, leaving a daughter, Margery, wife of Maurice de Stanlinch' and two sons, Henry, his heir, and Thomas, who became "jure uxous Isoldas de Cardinan," of Restormel Castle, Coonwall, Henry de Tracy's eldest son.

Henry de Tracy, of Toddington, appears in a charter, July 26, 1260, and was summoned to perform military service at Carmarthen, 11 Edward I. He died aria, 1296, and was succeeded by his son,

Sir William Tracy, of Toddington, who is recorded among the knights of the same county, in the 17th Edward I, and with

Ralph de Sudeley, his kinsman, is stated to have had a command in the Scottish war. He left a son and heir.

Sir William Tracy, of Toddington, who was in ward to Lawrence Tresham, 27 Edward I, at which time he is certified to hold £40 in lands. In the beginning of the reign of Edward II, he was at the tournament at Dunstable, as appears by an old drawing of a knight in armour, bearing a standard with the arms of the family. In the 17th of Edward II, he was, jointly with John Bermansel, high sheriff of Gloucestershire, which office in those times was of great authority. In a roll of the nobles of England, dated June 30, 1315, at Berwick, appear the names of this William Tracy, William de Sudeley, William le Boteler, of Wenun, etc. Sir William left a daughter, Margery, wife of John Archer, of Umbesslade, and a son and heir,

William Tracy, Esq., of Toddington, to whom, in conjunction with Thomas Berkeley, of Coberle, a mandate was issued, 7 Edward III, to raise three hundred men from the forest of Dene, and two hundred men from the county of Gloucester. His son and heir,

Sir John Tracy, of Toddington, knight of the shire of Gloucestershire, £2 Edward III, and sheriff for five years in succession, commencing in 1358, died in 1363, leaving, with a daughter, Margaret, wife of Sir Thomas de Langley, Knt., two sons, of whom the elder,

Sir John Tracy, of Toddington, M. P., and sheriff of Gloucestershire; died in 1379, leaving a daughter, Margaret, wife of Robert FitzElys, and a son and successor,

William Tracy, Esq., of Toddington, high sheriff in 1395; died in 1399. His son and heir,

William Tracy, Esq., of Toddington, was called to the privy council of Henry VI, as appears by private letters, still extant, written by the king in the most flattering terms, and dated July 21, 1401, "from my manor of Sutton." He was high sheriff 5 Henry V, and "one of those persons of quality in the county of Gloucester, who, bearing ancient arms from his ancestors, and holding by tenure, had summons in the 7 Henry V, to serve the king in person in defence of the realm." William Tracy, the privy councillor, married Alice, eldest daughter and co-heir of Sir Guy de la Spine, Knt., Lord of Coughton, county Warwick, and widow of William Gifford, (which Sir Guy de la Spine, was great grand-son of William de la Spine, by Joan, his wife, daughter and heir of Sir Simon Cocton, Knt.) and had issue, William his heir; John; Alice, who married Hugh Culme, Esq., of Moland, Devon. The elder son,

William Tracy, Esq., of Toddington, sheriff of Gloucestershire, 22 and 23 Henry VI, who married Margery, daughter of Sir John Pauncefort, Knt.; and died in 1460, leaving a daughter Margery, wife of Thomas Mylle, Esq., of Horscombe, county Salop, and two sons, Henry and Richard, the elder,

Henry Tracy, Esq., of Toddington, married Alice, daughter and co-heir of Thomas Baldington, Esq., of Alderly, county Oxon and died about 1506, leaving issue, two daughters, Anne married first, William Wye, second Thomas Mannington; Elizabeth, married first, Mr. Langley, second Sir Alexander Baynham; and three sons, viz: William, his heir; Richard, who married and had issue; and Ralph, a monk. The eldest son,

Sir William Tracy, of Toddington, was sheriff of Gloucestershire, in the 5 Henry VIII, anno, 1513. He was a gentleman of excellent parts and sound learning, and is memorable for being one of the first who embraced the reformed religion in England, as appears by his last will, dated 22 Henry VIII, which was condemned in the Bishop of London's Court after his decease, and an order sent to Parker, Chancellor of Worcester, to raise his body; but he too officiously burning the corpse, the recorder only warranting him to raise the body according to the law of the church, he was afterwards fined £400, and turned out of the chancellorship. Sir William's famous will is a curious document—most characteristic of the times. Sir William married Margaret, daughter of Sir Thomas Throckmorton of Corse Court, in Gloucestershire, and had issue: William, his heir; Richard, who obtained from his father the manor of Stanway, in the county of Gloucester, part of the lands of the Abbey of Tewksbury, which came to him by grant from the crown. "This Richard," says an old writer, "was well educated and wrote learnedly of his father's faith several treatises in the English tongue, and that most remarkable one, entitled "Preparations for the Cross," written experimentally, having suffered much in his estate for his fathers' reputed heretical will; he also wrote prophetically, of anno, 1550, (a few years before the beginning of Queen Mary) another treatise, "To Teach one to Die," which is annexed to his "Preparations for the Cross," which was printed, and falsely ascribed by the editor to be composed by John Frith, being one of the three that was found in the belly of a cod, brought into the market to be sold at Cambridge, A. D. 1626, wrapped about with canvass, very probably what that voracious fish plundered out of the pocket of some ship-wrecked seaman." In the 2nd of Elizabeth, he was sheriff of Gloucestershire, and having married Barbara, daughter of Thomas Lucy, Esq., of Charlecote, had three daughters and three sons, Paul, Nathaniel and Samuel. He was succeeded by the eldest,

Paul Tracy, Esq., of Stanway, in the county of Gloucester, high sheriff in the 20th of Elizabeth, who was created a baronet by King James I, June 29, 1611. Sir Paul married Anne, daughter of Ralph Shakerly, Esq., and had ten sons and as many daughters, of whom,

Richard, (Sir) the eldest, succeeded his father; Anne, married to Edward Hall, Esq., of the county of Worcester; Lucy, married to Ray Aylworth, Esq., of Aylworth, in the county of Gloucester; Alice: Hester, married to Francis, eldest son of John Kyrle, Esq., of Much Marcle, in Herefordshire; Elizabeth; Susan, married to William Price, Esq., of Winchester; Barbara; Margaret. He died about 1626, and was succeeded by his eldest son,

Sir Richard Tracy, who had received the honor of knighthood in the life-time of his father, and was sheriff of Gloucestershire, in the 4th of Queen Mary. He married Anne, daughter of Sir Thomas Coningsly, of Hampton, in the county of Hereford, and had three sons, Humphrey, Richard and John. He died about the year 1637, and was succeeded by the eldest

Sir Humphrey Tracy, sheriff of Gloucestershire in the 15th of Charles I, who suffered severely for his loyalty during the rebellion, having had to pay to sequestrators £1600 for compensation for his estate. He died without issue, and was succeeded by his brother, in 1651,

Sir Richard Tracy, who likewise died, (sine prole) without issue, and was succeeded about 1666, by his only surviving brother,

Sir John Tracy, who died issueless in 1677, when the baronetcy expired. 3 Robert, died without issue, (sine prole.) 1 Margaret, married to Richard Dyneley, Esq., of Charleton, county of Worcester. 2 Alice, married to ——— Wogan, Esq. The eldest son,

William Tracy, Esq., of Toddington, married Agnes, daughter of Sir Simon Digby, of Coleshill, county Warwick, and had (with two daughters, Margery, married to John Stratford, Esq., and Margaret, married to John Washbourne, Esq., of Wychynford) a son and successor,

Henry Tracy, Esq., of Toddington, who married Elizabeth, daughter of John Bruges, first Lord Chandos, of Sudeley, and died in 1557, (will dated Feb. 5, 1556, and proved in 1557) left issue: John, his heir; Giles, married Katherine Pickhurst, and had issue; Edward; Francis; Nicholas; Eleanor, married to Anthony Kingston, Esq. The eldest son,

Sir John Tracy, of Toddington, sheriff of and M. P. for Gloucestershire, was knighted by Queen Elizabeth in 1574. He married Anne, daughter of Sir Thomas Throckmorton, of Corse Court, and by her, (who died May 21, 1551) had, with other issue: John, (Sir) his heir; William, who married Mary, daughter of Sir John Conway, Knt. of Arrow; Thomas, (Sir) grand usher to the Queen, died without issue, (sine prole;) Mary, married first,

William Hoby, Esq., second, Horatio, Lord Vere, of Toddington, the famous general. Sir John died in 1591, and was succeeded by his son,

Sir John Tracy, of Toddington, who received knighthood from King James I, in 1609, and was advanced by letters-patent, dated Jan. 12, 1642, to the peerage of Ireland, as (Baron and Viscount Tracy, of Rathcole.) He married Anne, daughter of Sir Thomas Shirley, Knt. of Isfield, county Sussex, and was succeeded at his decease, by his son,

Robert Tracy, 2nd Viscount Tracy, was knighted by King Charles I, and sat in parliament as member for Gloucestershire. His lordship married first, Bridget, daughter of John Lyttleton, Esq., of Frankley Court, county Worcester, by Meriel, his wife, daughter of Sir Thomas Bromley, Lord Chancellor, and by her, (who died in 1632) had issue:

John, his heir; Robert, d. s. p.; Thomas, d. s. p.; William, d. s. p.;

Anne, who married William Somerville, Esq., of Edston, county Warwick, and was grand-mother of the author of "The Chase," and other poems; Meriel, married Sir William Poole, of Saperton; Frances, married Dr. Hinckley; Mary, died unmarried. His lordship married secondly, Dorothy, daughter of Thomas Cocks, Esq., of Castleditch, county Hereford, and had by her,

Robert, of Coscomb, one of the judges of the Court of King's Bench, and a commissioner of the Great Seal; married Anne, daughter of William Dowdeswell, Esq., of Pull Court, county Worcester, and died Sept. 11, 1735, aged 80, having had issue:

Richard, of Coscomb, who married Margaret, daughter of Owen Salusbury, Esq., of Rug, county Merioneth; and left at his decease, in 1734, an only child, Robert, of Coscomb, who died (sine prole) without issue, in 1756: Robert, of the Middle Temple, died unmarried, 1732;

Dorothy, married John Pratt, Esq.: Anne, married first, Charles Dowdeswell, Esq., of Forthampton Court, county Gloucester, second, Charles Wilde, Esq.; 2, Benjamin;

Dorothy, married William Higford, Esq., of Dixton, county Gloucester. The second viscount died in 1662, and was succeeded by his eldest son,

John Tracy, third viscount, who married Elizabeth, eldest surviving daughter of Thomas, first Lord Leigh, of Stoneleigh, and by her, (who died in 1688) had, with a daughter, the wife of Sir John Every, three sons, viz: William, his heir; Charles, died unmarried, May 3, 1676; Ferdinando, born in 1659, who became possessed of Stanway by the will of Sir John Tracy, last baronet of that branch. He married in 1680, Katherine, daughter of Sir Anthony Keck, and died in 1682, leaving an only child.

John, of Stanway, who married Anne, only daughter of Sir Robert Atkyns, of Saperton, chief Baron of the Exchequer; and died in 1735, leaving issue:

Robert, M. P., died without issue, (sine prole); Anthony, who assumed the surname of Keck, he married Lady Susan Hamilton, daughter of James, fourth Duke of Hamilton, and died May 30, 1769, left two daughters, Henrietta Charlotte, married Edward, Viscount Hereford, and Susan, married in 1771, Francis, Lord Elcho, and was mother of the seventh Earl of Wemyss; Thomas, of Sandywell, M. P., died issueless; John, who assumed the surname of Atkyns, and was Cursitor Baron of the Exchequer, died without issue; Anne, married John Travell, Esq.; Frances, married Gustavus Guy Dickens, Esq., colonel of the third regiment of Guards. His lordship was succeeded by his eldest son,

William Tracy, fourth viscount, who married first, Frances, daughter of Leicester Devereux, six viscount Hereford, by whom he had an only daughter, Elizabeth, married first Robert Burdet, Esq., secondly, Ralph Holden, Esq., of Aston, county Derby. His lordship married secondly, Jane, third daughter of the Hon. Sir Thomas Leigh, son of Thomas, second Lord Leigh, and died in 1712, leaving by her a daughter, Anne, married Sir William Keyt, Bart., and a son and heir,

Thomas Charles Tracy, fifth viscount, who married first, Elizabeth, eldest daughter of William Keyt, Esq., son of Sir William Keyt, Bart., of Edrington, and by her, (who died in 1719) had issue: William, died without issue, vita patris, 1752; Thomas Charles, sixth viscount; Jane, who married, Oct. 7, 1743, Capel Hanbury, Esq., of Pontypool Park. M. P. for Monmouthshire; and died March 7, 1787, leaving issue. Lord Tracy married secondly, Frances, eldest daughter of Sir John Pakington, Bart., of Westwood, county Worcester, and by her, (who died April 23, 1751) had issue: John, successor to his half-brother as seventh viscount; Robert Pakington died without issue, (sine prole) at Bombay, in 1748; Henry, eighth viscount; Frances, bed-chamber woman to Queen Charlotte, died unmarried; Anne, married June 23, 1757, to John Smith, Esq., of Combhay, county Somerset, who died in 1763; Dorothy, died young; Elizabeth, died young. The fifth viscount died June 4, 1756, and was succeeded by his eldest son,

Thomas Charles Tracy, sixth viscount. D. C. L., born in July, 1719, married Feb, 10, 1755, Harriet, daughter of Peter Bathurst, Esq., of Clarendon Park, Wilts, by the Lady Selina Shirly, his wife, daughter of Robert, Earl Ferrers, but died sine prole, Aug. 10, 1792, and was succeeded by his half-brother,

John Tracy, seventh viscount, warden of All Souls College, Oxford, at whose decease, unmarried in 1793, aged seventy-one, the houses and estates passed to his brother,

Henry Tracy, eighth viscount, born Jan. 25, 1732, married Dec. 12, 1767, Susannah, daughter of Anthony Weaver, Esq., of Morvil, county Salop, son of A. Weaver, Esq., M. D., of Castle House, Bridgenorth, who was brother of John Weaver, Esq., of Morvil, M. P., and of Anne Weaver, wife of John Blayney, Esq., of Cregyunog, county Montgomery, and mother of the late Arthur Blayney, Esq., of Gregyunog, who died unmarried October, 1795. By Susannah, his wife, (who died in 1783,) Lord Tracy left at his decease, April 27, 1797, an only surviving child and heiress,

The Hon. Henrietta Susannah Tracy, born Nov. 30, 1776, married Dec. 29, 1798, her cousin, Charles Hanbury, Esq., who had assumed by royal license, Dec. 10, previously, the additional surname and arms of Tracy, and who, having been raised to the peerage in 1838, was the first Baron Sudeley, of Toddington.

Family of Hanbury.

This family and that of Lord Bateman, derive from the same source, viz: the ancient house of Hanbury, of Hanbury, an old Worcestershire stock, which had been there seated, from a very remote period.

Henry de Hanbury, son of Geoffrey de Hanbury, of Hanbury, and grand-son of Geoffrey de Hanbury, living at Hanbury, temp. John was lord chief justice of the common pleas, in Ireland, temp. Edward II, and died about the year 1353. His son and heir,

Reginald de Hanbury, M. P. for Worcestershire, 37 Edward III, was father of

Roger de Hanbury, M. P. for Worcestershire, living at Hanbury, temp. Richard II, whose son and successor,

John de Hanbury, of Hanbury, A. D. 1430, married and had issue:

William, of Hanbury Hall, father, by Margery, his wife, of John Hanbury, Esq., of Hanbury Hall, county Worcester, ancestor of the Hanbury's of that place; John, of Beanhall, manor of Fakenham, county Worcester, whose son, Edward Hanbury, Esq., of Beanhall, was ancestor of the Hanbury's of Kelmarsh, whose heir male and representative, is Lord Bateman; Richard, of whose descendants we treat. The third son,

Richard Hanbury, Esq., married, and was father of

Richard Hanbury, Esq., who married, first, Catherine Smyth and secondly, Margery Tynter; by the former he was father of

Richard Hanbury, Esq., of Elmley Lovett, county Worcester, whose wife was a daughter of Basset, and whose son and heir,

John Hanbury, Esq., was of Elmly Lovett. He married twice, and by his second wife, a daughter of Bradley, was the father of

Richard Hanbury, Esq., of Elmley Lovett, who married Margery, daughter of Francis Bradley, Esq., and left a son and heir,

John Hanbury, Esq., of Fakenham, county Worcester, M. P. for the city of Gloucester in 1626, was a stanch parliamentarian, high in the confidence of Oliver Cromwell, by whom he was appointed sheriff of Worcester in 1649-50. He married Anne daughter of Christopher Capel, Esq., of Capel House, in Herefordshire, Alderman and M. P. for Gloucester; and died in 1659, left several children, of whom the youngest son,

Capel Hanbury, Esq., of Gloucester and of Whorestine, in Worcestershire, died in 1707, leaving by his first wife, (with a daughter Mary, wife of Mr. Sergeant John Hoo) a son and successor,

John Hanbury, Esq., of Pontypool Park, in Monmouthshire, M. P. for that county, and a major in the army; who married in July, 1703, Bridget, eldest daughter and co-heir of Sir Edward Ayscough, of Stallinborough, county Lincoln, and died June 13, 1734, leaving, (with other children, who died without issue,)

Capel, of whom presently: Charles (Sir) K. B. of Coldbrook Park, county Monmouth, born Dec. 8, 1709, M. P. for Monmouth, married in July, 1732, Frances, second daughter and co-heir of Thomas, Earl of Coningsly, and had two daughters, his co-heirs: Frances, married in 1754, to William, fourth Earl of Essex; Charlotte, married in 1750, to Hon. Robert Boyle. Sir Charles, who assumed the surname of Williams, died Nov. 17, 1759; George, of Coldbrook, born Sept. 23, 1715, who assumed the surname of Williams, at the decease of his brother, Sir Charles Hanbury-Williams. He married Margaret, daughter of John Chambre, Esq., of Llanfoist, county Monmouth, and died Dec. 11, 1764, leaving issue: Thomas, died in 1778, leaving issue. The eldest son, (to leave issue,)

Capel Hanbury, Esq., of Pontypool Park, M. P. for Monmouthshire, born Dec. 9, 1707, married Oct. 7, 1743, Jane, who died Aug. 13, 1744, daughter of Thomas Charles, fifth viscount Tracy, and died Dec. 7, 1765, left, with two daughters, Henrietta and Frances, (who both died unmarried) one son,

John Hanbury, Esq., of Pontypool Park, M. P. for the county Monmouth, born Aug. 1774, who married Jane, daughter of Morgan Lewis, Esq., of St. Pierre, in that shire, and by her, (who married secondly, Thomas Stoughton, Esq., of Ballyhorgan, county Kerry) had issue:

John Capel, born Jan. 27, 1775, died unmarried, aged 21, Dec. 1790; Capel, of Pontypool Park, Lord Lieutenant, county Monmouth, born Oct. 6, 1776, who assumed in 1797, the surname and arms of Leigh. He married first, April, 1797, Molly Anne, only daughter of Nathaniel Meyers, Esq., of Neath, Glamorganshire, and relict of Sir R. H. Mackworth, Bart., which lady died without issue, June 27, 1846. Mr. Hanbury-Leigh married secondly, Aug. 20, 1847, Emma Elizabeth, fourth daughter of Thomas Bates-Rous, Esq., of Courtyrala, county Glamorgan, and died Sept. 28, 1861, leaving issue by her; John Capel Hanbury, Esq., of Pontypool, born May 14, 1853, married Jan. 8, 1885, Louisa Charlotte, daughter of Col. Edward Eager; Emma and Frances Elizabeth, married Dec. 12, 1868, the Hon. A. L. G. Ashley, and died Aug. 2, 1875; Charles, first Lord Sudeley. Mr. Hanbury died April 4, 1784. His third son,

Charles Hanbury, Esq., of Toddington, county Gloucester, Lord Lieutenant of Montgomeryshire, born Dec. 28, 1777, married Dec. 29, 1798, Henrietta Susanna, only child and heir of Henry, eighth Viscount Tracy, and assumed in consequence the surname and arms of Tracy. By her, (who died June 5) his lordship had issue; Thomas Charles, second baron; Henry, born April 11, 1812, married Jan. 19,1841, Miss Rosamond Anne Myrtle-Shirley, daughter of the late Viscount Tamworth, and by her, (who died April 2) had issue: Charles Henry Tamworth, born Jan. 14, 1842; Arthur, born June 30, died Sept. 4, 1856;

Rosa Mary; Henrietta Susanna; John Capel, born Aug. 19, 1803, died May 4, 1852; Capel Arthur, in the E. I. Co's. civil service, born Jan. 5, 1809, married Sept. 18, 1833, Eliza Anne, daughter of Lieut. Col. John Tyler, R. A.; and died without issue, July 28, 1834. His widow married Capt. Graham, and died in 1837; William, late in the Madras civil service, born Jan. 18, 1810; Edward, (Rev.) born Feb. 6, 1812, chaplain to H. M's. Embassy at Vienna, 1848-1856; Henrietta; Frances died Dec. 23, 1867; Laura Susanna, died June 30, 1881. His lordship was raised to the peerage as Baron Sudeley, of Toddington, July 12, 1838. He died Feb. 10, 1858, and was succeeded by his eldest son,

Thomas Charles, 2nd baron, who was born Feb. 5, 1801, and married Aug. 25, 1831, Emma Elizabeth Alicia, second daughter of the late George Hay-Dawking-Pennant, Esq., of Penrhyn Castle, county Carnarvon, by Sophia Mary, his wife, daughter of the first Viscount Hawarden, and had issue: Sudeley-Charles-George, third baron; Charles-Douglas-Richard, present peer; Algernon-Cornwallis-Henry, born March 21, 1844, died Feb. 8, 1845; Alfred-Francis-Algernon, M. A. Rev., vicar of Dymock, county Gloucester, born Oct. 13, 1846, married April 11, 1868, Agnes Jane, eldest daughter of Henry James Hoare, Esq., of Morden Lodge, Surry, and has, Bertram-Henry-Algernon, born July 21, 1875; Una-Theodora-Alicia, born Jan. 12, 1870; and Sybil-Mary-Alice, born June 22, 1873; Frederick-Stephen-Archibald, M. P. for Montgomery, (116, Queen's Gate, S. W.) born Sept. 15, 1848, married Sept. 8, 1870, Helena-Caroline, daughter of Sir Thomas E. Winnington, Bart., and has issue: Eric-Thomas-Henry, born July 4, 1871; Claud-Sudeley-Francis, born Nov. 3, 1873, died May 12, 1874; Edith-Julia-Helena, born Sept. 2, 1872; Cyprienne-Emma-Madeline, born Oct. 27, 1874; Violet-Mary-Claudia, born Feb. 27, 1876; Hilda-Adelaide-Eleanor, born July 16, 1877; Gwyneth-Rose-Goda, born Sept. 20, 1879; Hubert-George-Edward, born Aug. 14, 1855; Juliana-Sophia-Elizabeth; Georgiana-Henrietta-Emma, married Oct. 6, 1859;

Charles-Henry-Maude, Esq., captain Madras army, and has issue: Adelaid-Frances-Isabella, married May 28, 1859, to the Rev. Frederick Peel, vicar of Malvern, Worcester, (see Peel, Bart.;) Alice-Augusta-Gertrude, married May 17, 1861, to Lieut. Col. Charles E. Webber, C. B., royal engineers, and died Feb. 25, 1877. t eir only daughter, Evelyn-Emma-Frances, died April 7, 1877; Gertrude-Emely-Rosamond, died an infant, Jan. 24, 1842; Madeline-Emily-Augusta, married Dec. 30, 1875, to the Hon. and Rev. Maurice Ponsonby, second son of Lord de Manley, and has issue. His lordship, who was lord-lieutenant of Montgomeryshire, died at Pau, Feb. 19, 1863, and was succeeded by his eldest son.

Sudeley-Charles-George, third baron, born April 9, 1837; lieutenant of county Montgomery, and for some time in the grenadier guards, in which corps he was appointed captain in 1857, and retired in 1863. His lordship died unmarried, April 28 1877, and was succeeded by his next brother, Charles-Douglas-Richard, fourth and present Baron Sudeley.

all of which stand for Tracy. The shell denotes that an ancestor went on a pilgrimage or crusade. The second and third parts are divided by a plain green band, with engrailed edge, (um) and narrow black border, for Hanbury.

CRESTS—On an ermine cap turned up, an escallop shell, black, between two wings of gold, for Tracy. Out of a sable mural crown, a golden demi-lion rampant, holding in the paws a black battle-axe, with helve of gold, for Hanbury.

SUPPORTERS—On either side a purple falcon, with wings extended, and beaks and bills of gold.

MOTTO—Memoria pii ætena—The memory of the good man is immortal—The memory of the just is eternal.

Badge of the Lords Sudeley—Crests—On a chapeau, turned up, ermine, an escallop. sa., between two wings, are for Tracy. Out of a mural crown, sa., a demi-lion, rampant, or holding in the paws a battle-axe, sa., helved gold, for Hanbury. Supporters—On either side a falcon, wings elevated, ppr., beaked and belled. Motto—Memoria pii æterna.

Seats—Toddington Park, Winchcombe, Gloucestershire, and Gregyunog, Newtown, county Montgomery. Clubs—Brook's, Traveler's Town-house—7 Buckingham Gate, S. W.

Sudeley, Viscount. see Arran, Earl of.

THE TRACY'S.

COPIED FROM NORWICH TOWN RECORDS OF BIRTHS, MARRIAGES, AND DEATHS.

John Tracy, born in 1642, married Mary Winslow, June 17, 1670. Their children were: Josiah Tracy, born Aug. 10, 1671, died Jan. 27, 1672; John Tracy, Jr., born Jan. 19, 1672; Elizabeth Tracy, born July 7, 1676; Joseph Tracy, born April 20, 1682; Winslow Tracy, born Feb. 9, 1688. Mr. John Tracy died Aug. 16, 1702. Mrs. Mary Tracy died July 31, 1721.

Lieut. Thomas Tracy died Nov. 7, 1685.

Jonathan Tracy married Mary Griswold, July 11, 1672. Their children were: Jonathan Tracy, Jr., born Feb. 21, 1674; Hannah Tracy, born July 8, 1677; Christopher Tracy, born May 1, 1680; Mary Tracy, born Sept. 7, 1682.

Jeremiah Tracy married Mary Witter, Oct. 13, 1713. Their children were: Mary Tracy, born Nov. 19, 1714; Ebenezer Tracy, born Oct. 29, 1716; Jeremiah Tracy, Jr., born April 19, 1719; Andrew Tracy, born Feb. 5, 1721; Dorothy Tracy, born May 5, 1724; Abiah Tracy, born Aug. 15, 1726, died Aug. 31, 1727; second Abiah Tracy, born Dec. 31, 1728; Elizabeth Tracy, born Jan. 21, 1731.

Winslow Tracy, born Feb. 9, 1688, married Rachel Ripley, June 21, 1714. Their children were: Joshua Tracy, born June 19, 1715, died Dec. 13, 1715; Percy Tracy, born Nov. 13, 1716; Josiah Tracy, born May 10, 1718; Elephlet Tracy, born Nov. 14, 1720; Nehemiah Tracy, born March 18, 1722; Samuel Tracy, born Dec. 5, 1724; Solomon Tracy, born May 22, 1728.

Isaac Clark married Meriam Tracy, May 27, 1707, had eight children.

John Tracy married Margaret Hyde. Their children were: John, born Feb. 11, 1726, at Norwich. married Margaret Huntington; Eleazer, born March 16, 1728, at Norwich, supposed to have been killed by the Indians in the French war; Josiah, born April 17, 1736; Hezekiah, born 1736, at Norwich; Daniel, born March 14, 1738, at Norwich; Theophilus, born Sept. 14, 1742, at Norwich; Joshua, born Aug. 13. 1745, at Norwich; Elizabeth, born May 1, 1747; Margaret, born May 16, 1749; Rachel, born Sept. 27, 1750.

Solomon Tracy married Sarah Huntington, Nov. 23, 1676. Their children were: Lydia Tracy, born Oct. 11, 1677; Simon Tracy, born Jan. 8, 1679. Mrs. Sarah Tracy, the wife of Solomon, died Aug. 31, 1683. Solomon Tracy married Sarah Solomon, relict of Thomas Solomon, April 8, 1688. Solomon Tracy died July 9, 1732. Mrs. Sarah Tracy died Aug. 29, 1730.

Samuel Tracy died Jan. 11, 1693.

Daniel Tracy married Abigail Adgate, Sept. 19, 1683. Their children were: Daniel Tracy, Jr,, born Dec. 7, 1682. Abigail Tracy died Sept. 23, 1710. Daniel Tracy married Hannah Bingham, widow of Thomas Bingham, March 4, 1711. Elizabeth Tracy, born Feb. 10, 1712, died April 16, 1715; Samuel Tracy, born March 12, 1714. Mr, Daniel Tracy died June 29, 1728.

Thomas Leffingwell married Lydia Tracy, March 11, 1698; had seven children.

John Tracy married Elizabeth Leffingwell, May 10, 1697. Their children were: Elizabeth Tracy, born April 16, 1698; John Tracy, Jr., born June 27, 1700; Hezekiah Tracy, born Aug. 30, 1702; Joshua Tracy, born Feb. 27, 1705, died April 28, 1705; Isaac Tracy, born May 25, 1706; Anna Tracy, born Nov. 29, 1708; Ruth Tracy, born Sept. 13, 1711. John Tracy, Sen., died March 27, 1729. Mrs. Elizabeth Tracy died Oct. 25, 1737. Elizabeth Leffingwell, wife of John Tracy, was the daughter of Thomas Leffingwell and Mary Bushnell,

Joseph Tracy, born April 20, 1682, married Mary Abel, Dec. 31, 1705. Their children were: Joseph Tracy, Jr., born Oct. 17,

1706; Mary Tracy, born June 4, 1707; Margaret Tracy, born May 11, 1710; Elisha Tracy, born May 17, 1712; Zerwich Tracy, born Dec. 14, 1714; Lydia Tracy, born Dec. 10, 1716; Irene Tracy, born Jan. 15, 1718; Phineas Tracy, born Jan. 1, 1720; Jerusha Tracy, born May 23, 1723. Capt. Joseph Tracy died April 10, 1765.

Simon Tracy, born Jan. 8, 1679, married Mary Leffingwell, Jan. 14, 1707. Their children were: Simon Tracy, born Nov. 24, 1709, died Feb. 29, 1710; second Simon Tracy, born Nov. 7, 1710; Civil Tracy, born Dec. 8, 1712; Moses Tracy, born Oct. 4, 1714; Job Tracy, born Jan. 11, 1716, died Oct. 5, 1719; Lydia Tracy, born June 12, 1719. Mrs. Mary Tracy died Sept. 23, 1770, aged 89 years. Mr. Simon Tracy died Sept. 14, 1775, aged 96 years.

The names of Joseph Tracy's children are as follows: Joseph Tracy, son of Joseph and Abigail, his wife, born April 22, 1725; Anna Tracy, born Feb. 5, 1726; John Tracy, born Sept. 2, 1729; Sarah Tracy, born Sept. 17, 1731; Asa Tracy, born Sept. 4, 1733; Elijah Tracy, born June 25, 1735; Jesse Tracy, born June 14, 1739, died young; second Jesse Tracy, born April 20, 1741.

Richard Hyde married Anna Tracy, Nov. 12, 1750, daughter of John Tracy and Elizabeth Leffingwell.

Daniel Tracy, Jr., married Abigail Leffingwell, March 14, 1710. Their children were: Abigail Tracy, born July 10, 1716, died May 4, 1725; Daniel Tracy, born Jan. 3, 1718, died June 1, 1728; Samuel Tracy, born Sept. 23, 1723; Hannah Tracy, born Sept. 2, 1727; second Daniel Tracy, born Oct. 24, 1730, died Nov. 2, 1739. Mr. Daniel Tracy died Jan. 29, 1771. Mrs. Abigail Tracy died March 16, 1777.

Isaac Tracy married Elizabeth Bushnell April 9, 1730. Their children were: Joseph Tracy, born May 17, 1731; Zerwich Tracy, born Oct. 5, 1735; Elizabeth Tracy, born Nov. 14, 1737; Ruth Tracy, born Oct. 10, 1739; Andrew Tracy, born Dec. 9, 1742; Zerwich Tracy, born Feb. 26, 1746, died Feb. 13, 1752;

Eunice Tracy, born Dec. 18, 1748; Hannah Tracy, born Jan. 14, 1750.

Civil Tracy married John Huntington, Nov. 5, 1735.

Ebenezer Tracy, son of Jeremiah Tracy and Mary his wife, died April 15, 1738. Stephen Tracy, son of Jeremiah Tracy and his wife, Mary, born Oct. 17, 1738. Abiah Tracy died Sept. 9, 1743. Stephen Tracy died Sept. 9. 1743. Dorothy Tracy died Oct. 6, 1743.

Simeon Tracy, Jr., married Elizabeth Hyde, daughter of Jabez Hyde, Dec. 29, 1735. Their children were: Elizabeth Tracy, born Sept., 1738; Jabez Tracy, born March 25, 1740; Mary Tracy, born Aug. 19, 1741. Elizabeth, wife of Simeon Tracy, Jr., died Aug. 22, 1741. Simeon Tracy, Jr., married Abigail Bushnell, his second wife, Nov. 23, 1724. Their children were: Abigail Tracy, born Dec. 9, 1744, died July 12, 1746; second Abigail Tracy, born Sept. 10, 1745; Mendator Tracy, born May 18, 1749; Simeon Tracy, born April 16, 1752, died Jan. 20, 1755. Abigail Tracy, wife of Simeon Tracy, Jr., died July 6, 1774.

Daniel Tracy married Dorothy Safford, Nov. 22, 1733. Their children were: Daniel Tracy, Jr., born July 1, 1734; John Tracy, born Oct. 8, 1736; Elisha Tracy, born Nov. 28, 1739; Minor Tracy, born Oct. 4, 1742; Desire Tracy, born Aug. 4, 1745; Nathaniel Tracy, born April 1, 1748; Olive Tracy, born July 27, 1751. Mr. Daniel Tracy died Nov. 8, 1760. This Daniel Tracy was son of Thomas Tracy, Jr. Olive Tracy married Daniel Witter in 1748. He died in 1781 and she died in 1814. They had one son, William, born in 1769, who died in 1811.

Joseph Tracy married Mary Fuller Feb. 14, 1736. Their children were: Mary Tracy, born Jan. 6, 1737, died Feb. 2, 1745; Ziporah Tracy, born March 30, 1740; Joseph Tracy, Jr., born June 1, 1741, died Aug. 7, 1746; Avery Tracy, born Feb. 24, 1742; Asher Tracy, born Aug. 14, 1744, died Sept. 13, 1744; Zerviah Tracy, born April 5, 1746; second Joseph Tracy, born Oct. 7, 1747; Mary Tracy, born May 10, 1749, died July 24, 1751;

Ebenezer Tracy, born Jan. 22, 1752; Lydia Tracy, born Aug. 25, 1752.

Moses Tracy, married Sarah Leffingwell, May 25, 1737. Their children were: David Tracy, born April 22, 1739; Zachariah Tracy, born March 6, 1742; Nathan Tracy, born Sept. 24, 1745; Moses Tracy, Jr., born March 1, 1747; Leander Tracy, born Jan. 2, 1750; Solomon Tracy, born March 5, 1756.

Joseph Tracy, Jr., married Anne Hinckley, of Lebanon. March 5, 1739. Their children were: Jarred Tracy, born Oct. 10, 1741; Ruby Tracy, born May 14, 1746, died July 9, 1751; Frederick Tracy, born Aug. 3, 1749; Anne Tracy, born Nov. 30, 1751; Uriah Tracy, born Aug. 9, 1753; Lois Tracy, born Aug. 19, 1755. Mr. Joseph Tracy died April 19, 1787.

Percy Tracy married Elizabeth Hyde, Aug. 7, 1740. Their children were: Joshua Tracy, born June 7, 1741; Richard Tracy, born Sept. 17, 1743; Elizabeth Tracy, born June 23, 1746; William Tracy, born May 2, 1750; Benjamin Tracy, born Nov. 4, 1756.

Josiah Tracy married Rachel Allen, Nov. 3, 1740. Their children were: Irene Tracy, born Dec. 21, 1741; Nehemiah Tracy, born March 23, 1744; Daniel Tracy, born Nov. 8, 1746, died Jan. 19, 1747; Anne Tracy, born Dec. 22, 1748; Dorothy Tracy, born Aug. 26, 1751; Calvin Tracy, born Sept. 14, 1753, died Jan. 1, 1755; second Daniel Tracy, born Oct. 23, 1756; second Calvin Tracy, born June 7, 1753. Rachel Allen died Aug. 8, 1761. Josiah Tracy married Esther Pride, second wife, June 28, 1762. Their children were: Rachel Tracy, born June 8, 1763, died Dec. 20, 1777; Mehetible Tracy, born Oct. 28, 1765.

Andrew Tracy married Ruth Smith, March 30, 1743. Their children were: Ebenezer Tracy, born April 20, 1744; Jesse Tracy born Dec. 31, 1745; Sarah Tracy, born Jan. 25, 1747; Andrew Tracy, Jr., born March 17, 1749; Elijah Tracy, born May 14, 1752, died Feb. 23, 1763; Ruth Tracy, born Oct. 1, 1754; Mary Tracy, born Sept. 9, 1756; Anne Tracy, born March 9, 1859;

Jeremiah Tracy, born April 11, 1761; Elizabeth Tracy, born Feb. 11, 1784; David Tracy, born May 25, 1766.

Margaret Tracy married William Waterman, Sept. 23, 1733, and had five children.

Elephelet Tracy married Sarah Manning, Dec. 16, 1742. Their children were: Elisha Tracy, born Feb. 23, 1743; Allatheu Tracy, born Jan. 28, 1746; Lucy Tracy, born Sept. 26, 1749; Uriah Tracy, born Feb. 3, 1755.

David Tracy, Jr., married Mrs. Eunice Elliot, April 18, 1744. Their children were: Silas Tracy, born March 27, 1745; Eunice Tracy, born April 23, 1752; Lemuel Tracy, born May 12, 1754. Mrs. Eunice Tracy died Oct. 4, 1756.

Elisha Tracy married Lucy Huntington, June 16, 1743. Their children were: Lucy Tracy, born July 20, 1744; Alice Tracy, born Oct. 11, 1745; Lucretia Tracy, born Sept. 5, 1747; Lydia Tracy, born Dec. 23, 1749; Philura Tracy, born Sept. 30, 1751. Mrs. Lucy Tracy, wife of Elisha Tracy, died in 1751. Elisha Tracy married Elizabeth Dorr, second wife, April 16, 1754. Phineas Tracy, born June 29, 1755; Philemon Tracy, born May 3, 1757; Elizabeth Tracy, born June 29, 1760, died Oct. 20, 1773; Charlotte Tracy, born May 27, 1762; Mary Tracy, born May 3, 1764; Elisha Tracy, Jr., born May 27, 1766; Joseph Winslow Tracy, born Aug. 11, 1769, died July 6, 1770; Deborah Dorr-Tracy, born Nov. 9, 1770.

Isaac Tracy married Elizabeth Bushnell. Their children were: Ebenezer Tracy, born April 19, 1754. Mrs. Elizabeth Tracy, wife of Isaac Tracy, died May 12, 1764. Eunice Tracy, daughter of Isaac Tracy, died April 18, 1767, (there is no record of the birth of Eunice on the book,) Ebenezer Tracy, son of Isaac Tracy, died May 23, 1769. Isaac Tracy died Jan. 25, 1779.

Jeremiah Tracy, Jr., married Abigail Storey, Feb. 6, 1746. Their children were: Dorothy Tracy, born Feb. 12, 1746, died March 6, 1747; Stephen Tracy, born Feb. 1, 1748; Abigail Tracy born Oct. 14, 1750. Mrs. Abigail Tracy, wife of Jeremiah Traey, Jr., died Dec. 14, 1750. Jeremiah Tracy, Jr., married Anne Cleveland, Aug. 27, 1751; Jeremiah Tracy, Jr., born Aug. 6, 1754, died Jan. 31, 1755. Jeremiah Tracy, Jr., married Margaret Huntington, May 17, 1755; Solomon Tracy, born May 1, 1756. Jeremiah Tracy died March 16, 1757.

John Tracy married Margaret Huntington, Oct. 13, 1747. Their children were: Mary Tracy, born April 1, 1750; Margaret Tracy, born May 29, 1753; John Tracy, born Dec. 21, 1755. Mrs. Margaret Tracy, wife of John, Jr., died Dec. 24, 1755. John Tracy, Jr., married Bethia Johnson, Jan. 16, 1758; Eleazer Tracy, born April 28, 1759, died July 7, 1759; second Eleazer Tracy, born June 28, 1790, died Oct. 7, 1760; Bethia Tracy, born April 14, 1754, died Sept. 2, 1764; Oliver Tracy, born Jan. 11, 1769; Erastus Tracy, born Feb. 14, 1771.

Samuel Tracy married Mrs. Sybel Lathrop, May 17, 1750. Their children were: Daniel Tracy, born June 8, 1751, died June 27, 1753; Sybel Tracy, born Aug. 2, 1753; second Daniel Tracy, born March 27, 1758; Zebediah Tracy, born April 26, 1759; Ebenezer Tracy, born Nov. 11, 1792; Abigail Tracy, born Jan. 18, 1765; Thomas Tracy, born Dec. 22, 1767. Mr. Daniel Tracy, son of Samuel Tracy, married Lucretia Hubbord, Nov. 5, 1782. Daniel Tracy, son of Samuel, died Dec. 6, 1782.

Nathaniel Tracy died March 12, 1751.

Lemuel Tracy married Sarah Williams July 16, 1752. Their children were: Mary Tracy, born Oct. 24, 1753; Sarah Tracy, born Dec. 23, 1755. Mr. Lemuel Tracy died July 14, 1756.

David Tracy married Abigail Cleveland, Jan. 10, 1753. Their children were: Elizabeth Tracy, born Sept. 29, 1753; David Tracy, Jr., born April 10, 1755.

Nehemiah Tracy married Meriam Waterman, Feb. 12, 1767.

Solomon Tracy married Mrs. Anne Edgerton, Sept. 1, 1755. Their children were: Sybel Tracy, born Aug. 5, 1756; Samuel Tracy, born March 4, 1758; Sarah Tracy, born June 3, 1761; Eleazer Tracy, born July 12, 1763; Louisa Tracy, born May 29,

1765; Winslow Tracy, born April 10, 1770; Clarissa Tracy, born April 18, 1773,

Samuel Tracy, son of Moses Tracy and wife, Esther, born June 3, 1758. Sybel Tracy, daughter of Moses Tracy and wife, Ester, born Sept. 8, 1760.

Josiah Tracy, Jr., Married Margaret Sette, Dec. 15, 1757. Their children were: Cynthia Tracy, born Sept. 6, 1758; Lucy Tracy, born Oct. 7, 1760: Margaret Tracy, born Dec. 14, 1762; Eleazer Tracy, born March 21, 1763; Peter Tracy, born April 19, 1767; Bethia Tracy, born July 10, 1769; Josiah Tracy, Jr., born May 7, 1772; Lucretia Tracy, born Sept. 4, 1774; Rachel Tracy, born March 6, 1777; Naoma Tracy, born March 17, 1780; Zebediah Tracy, born July 18, 1782.

Hezekiah Tracy, Jr., married Elizabeth Pettis, Aug. 9, 1759, Their children were: Dudley Tracy, born Sept. 28, 1759; Elizabeth Tracy, born Dec. 1, 1762; Welthea Tracy, born Feb. 13, 1767; Joshua Tracy, born Oct. 16, 1768; Hezekieh Tracy, born May 5, 1771.

Daniel Tracy, third, married Mary Johnson, of Norwich, Sept. 16, 1762. Their children were: Uriah Tracy, born Feb. 8, 1774; Hiel Tracy, born July 5, 1765; James Tracy, born May 3, 1770; Mary Tracy, born Sept. 22, 1772; Daniel Tracy, born Aug. 3, 1774.

Alethea Tracy married Asahel Smith, Sept. 23, 1767, and had six children.

Jabez Tracy married Ziporah Hebard, May 26, 1763. Their children were: Jabez Tracy, Jr., born Oct. 21, 1764; Elizabeth Tracy, born June 8, 1768. Mrs. Ziporah Tracy died Feb. 26, 1769. Jabez Tracy married Hannah Edgerton, June 26, 1776; Simeon Tracy, born Feb. 10, 1777; Hannah Tracy, born Nov. 5, 1778.

Daniel Tracy, fourth, married Anna Lamb, July 12, 1764. Their children were: Lucinda Tracy, born June 20, 1765; Dorastus Tracy, born July 28, 1766: Lysanias Tracy, born Jan. 31,

1768; Arza Tracy, born July 21, 1771; Philanea Tracy, born June 18, 1775.

Andrew Tracy, Jr., married Mrs. Molly Clement, Nov. 27, 1765. Their children were: Peleg Tracy, born Sept. 25, 1776; Leonard Tracy, born Jan. 19, 1770; Molly Tracy, born Dec. 27, 1771; Zebediah Tracy, born Nov. 16, 1774; Eunice Tracy, born July 22, 1776; Elizabeth Backus-Tracy, born March 21, 1779; Sidney Tracy, born May 25, 1781; Harriet Tracy, born April 4, 1783.

Jarred Tracy married Margaret Grant, Oct. 20, 1765. Their children were: Sarah Tracy, born Feb. 10, 1768; William Gidney-Tracy, born Nov. 15, 1768; Susannah Tracy, born Aug. 8, 1770; Joseph Winslow Tracy, born March 9, 1773; Gardner Tracy, born Feb. 23, 1777; James Grant Tracy, born March 16, 1781; Margaret Tracy, born Dec. 19, 1783, died March 24, 1783.

Theophilus Tracy married Sarah Gifford, Dec. 10, 1766. Their children were: Theophilus Tracy, born Nov. 16, 1768; Sarah Tracy, born Dec. 15, 1770; Experience Tracy, born Dec. 16, 1772; Riel Tracy, born Dec. 5, 1774; Stephen Tracy, born Nov. 4, 1776; Welthea Tracy, born Oct. 2, 1778; Anna Tracy, born Oct. 6, 1780; Hannah Tracy, born June 20, 1783; Ruth Tracy, born May 16, 1785.

Nehemiah Tracy married Miriam Waterman, February 12, 1767.

Ebenezer Tracy married Mary Freeman, May 15, 1765. Their children were: Elijah Tracy, born April 17, 1766; Ziporah Tracy, born July 21, 1769; Mary Tracy, born January 15, 1770.

Jesse Tracy married Faith Bingham, Sept. 27, 1770. Their children were: Lucy Tracy, born Aug. 2, 1771; Jesse Tracy, born Oct. 4, 1773; Freeman Tracy, born March 5, 1775; Hannah Tracy, born March 24, 1777; Jedediah Tracy, born June 12, 1779; Faith Tracy, born Aug. 6, 1781; Andrew Tracy, born Nov.

16, 1783; Erastus Tracy, born Nov. 17, 1785; Felix Tracy and Anna Tracy, not on the Town Records.

Elisha Tracy married Dorothy Wilson, Nov. 7, 1771. Their children were: Guredon Tracy, born Sept. 12, 1772; Molly Tracy, born Dec. 10, 1775.

Andrew Tracy, Jr., married Anna Bingham, Sept. 17, 1773. Their children were: Lemuel Tracy, born July 29, 1773; Ruth Tracy, born March 30, 1775; Lucy Tracy, born Nov. 4, 1777; Elias Tracy, born Jan. 22, 1780; Stephen Tracy, born July 2, 1782.

Mendator Tracy married Caroline Bushnell, Oct. 28, 1773. Their children were: Caroline Tracy, born Jan. 14, 1776, died Dec. 1, 1781; Phebe Tracy, born Jan. 6, 1779; Simeon Tracy, born Sept. 14, 1781; Jedediah Tracy, born Feb. 15, 1784. Mrs. Caroline Tracy died Jan. 25, 1785. Mendator Tracy married Nabby Lord, May 4, 1785.

Joshua Tracy married Naoma Bingham, May 22, 1771. Their children were: Abel Tracy, born April 26, 1772; Thomas Tracy, born May 23, 1774; Joshua Tracy, Jr., born Dec. 21, 1776, died May 11, 1779. Mr. Joshua Tracy died March 26, 1777.

Samuel Tracy, third, married Hannah Storey, July 3, 1780. Their children were: Olford Tracy, born Feb. 17, 1781; Samuel Tracy, born Dec. 25, 1782.

John Tracy, fourth, married Esther Pride, May 24, 1781.

Calvin Tracy married Elizabeth Huntington, Dec. 13, 1781. Their children were: Anna Huntington-Tracy, born Jan. 12, 1783; Calvin Tracy, Jr., born March 16, 1784.

Daniel Tracy, son of Josiah, married Lucy Tracy, Oct. 30, 1783. Their children were: Lucy Tracy, born Sept. 13, 1784; Nancy Tracy, born Aug. 18, 1786.

David Tracy married Susannah Capron, Dec. 3, 1789. Their children were: David Tracy, Jr., born March 9, 1791; Susannah Tracy, born Jan. 21, 1793; Betsey Tracy, born May 16, 1795; Charles Tracy, born Nov. 14, 1796; Mary Tracy, born May 19, 1800; Mary Ann Tracy, born June 20, 1802; George Tracy, born

Dec. 11, 1804; William Tracy, born June 2, 1807; Sarah Tracy, born June 12, 1811.

Nathan Tracy married Hannah Kingsley, Oct. 1769. Their children were: Civil Tracy, born May 21, 1772; Sally Tracy, born July 15, 1774; Hannah Tracy, born Sept. 3, 1776; Nathan Tracy, born Feb. 16, 1779; Clarissa Tracy, born April 1, 1781; Lucy Tracy, born March 21, 1788. Mrs. Hannah Tracy died April 4, 1788, aged 44 years.

Uriah Tracy married Lydia Hullman, Feb. 9, 1794. Their children were: William George Tracy, born Jan. 11, 1797.

Barton Tracy married Betsey Case, April 1, 1798. Their children were: Lucy Tracy, born Oct. 29, 1798; Luther Tracy, born June 12, 1800; Elisha Tracy, born April 19, 1802.

Benjamin Tracy married Hannah Johnson, of Bozrah, May 22, 1806.

Joseph Winslow Tracy, married Wealthy Huntington, of Bozrah, Sept. 21, 1807. Their children were: Jarred Winslow Tracy, born May 29, 1812; James Joseph Tracy, born Dec. 3, 1814; Edward Huntington Tracy, born April 21, 1817; Sarah Grant Tracy, born Aug. 21, 1819; Cornelia Margaretta Tracy, born Oct. 15, 1822; Lydia Huntington Tracy, born July 3, 1825.

Dorastus Tracy married Lovice Sanford, Nov. 16, 1788. Their children were: Charles Tracy, born Feb. 18, 1790, died Sept. 18, 1806; Fanney Tracy, born Nov. 13, 1792; Elisha Tracy, born May 11, 1794; Harvy Tracy, born July 17, 1796; Lovice Tracy, born June 1, 1798; Almira Tracy, born **May 28, 1800**; Jabez Tracy, born March 2, 1803, died May 3, 1804; Eliza Tracy, born Feb. 8, 1805; William Sanford Tracy, born March 22, 1809; Sophrona Tracy, born Sept. 17, 1811; Mary Ann Tracy, born Dec. 7, 1813.

Jedediah Tracy married Mercy M. Doan, Oct., 29, 1812. Their children were: Caroline Abbey Tracy, born March 24, 1815.

Elisha Tracy married Lucy Coit Huntington, Oct. 31, 1796. Their children were: William Swan Tracy, born Feb. 4, 1799; Winslow Tracy, born Jan. 13, 1801; Elizabeth Dorr Tracy, born

July 22, 1813; Lucy Huntington Tracy, born May 11, 1806; Hannah Phelps Tracy, born April 13, 1808, died Feb. 13, 1810; Elisha Dorr Tracy, born June 4, 1811; Stephen Decatur Tracy, born July 14, 1813.

Nathaniel Tracy married Fanney Kelley, Nov. 15, 1807. Their children were: Fanney Tracy, born June 17, 1808; Caroline Tracy, born June 27, 1810; John Tracy, born Jan. 12, 1813; Daniel Tracy, born Sept, 7, 1818; Lucy Tracy, born March 7, 1821·

Joshua Tracy married Hannah H. Mansfield, March 28, 1810. Their children were: Juliet Tracy, born Dec. 30, 1810; died Feb. 12, 1815; Augustus Converse Tracy, born Feb. 13, 1812, died Dec. 19. 1814; James Lawrence Tracy, born July 2, 1813; Caroline Mansfield Tracy, born July 24, 1814; Joshua Perkins Tracy, born March 31, 1816, died Nov. 13, 1816. Joshua Tracy died Aug. 10, 1816.

———o———

The Tracy-Preston Record.

Jonathan Tracy and Mary Griswold were married July 11, 1672. Their children were: Jonathan Tracy, born Feb. 21, 1675; Hannah Tracy, born July 8, 1677; Christopher Tracy, born March 1, 1680; Mary Tracy born Sept. 7, 1682; Maryam Tracy, born April 23, 1685; David Tracy, born Sept. 4, 1687; Frances Tracy, born April 1, 1690; Sarah Tracy, born Aug. 2, 1692, died Sept. 6, 1693; Samuel Tracy, born June 6, 1697; Jonathan Tracy, Jr., died Feb. 25, 1704. Mary Tracy, the wife of Jonathan Tracy, Sen., died April 24, 1711, in the 55th year of her age.

Jonathan Tracy and Mary Richard were married Aug. 21, 1711.

Hannah Tracy and Thomas Davison were married Nov. 28, 1695.

Jedediah Tracy and Margaret Rix were married Jan. 27, 1714. Their children were: Jedediah Tracy, born Dec. 17, 1714; Charity Tracy, born Dec. 23, 1716; Margaret Tracy, born Oct. 27, 1718; Sarah Tracy, born Sept. 23, 1720; Abigail Tracy, born March 23, 1722; Thomas Tracy, born Sept. 3, 1724; Mary Tracy, born July 16, 1726. Margaret Tracy, wife of Jedediah Tracy, died Aug. 1, 1727. The above named Jedediah Tracy was married to Mary Parke, April 15, 1728. Their children were: Caswell Tracy, born Sept. 10, 1730; Benjamin Tracy, born Nov. 6, 1739.

Jonathan Tracy and Anna Palmer were married Feb. 11, 1700. Their children were: Jonathan Tracy, born Nov. 30, 1702; Anna Tracy, born Oct. 29, 1703. Jonathan Tracy, Sen., died Feb. 25, 1704.

Jeremiah Tracy and Mary Witter were married Oct. 13, 1713.

Francis Tracy and Elizabeth Parrish were married Jan. 6, 1713. Their children were: Elizabeth Tracy, born August 23, 1714; Isaac Tracy, born Nov. 9, 1716; Frances Tracy, born Feb. 23, 1717; Thankful Tracy, born Nov. 29, 1718; Menum Tracy, born Oct. 12, 1720; Sheribiah Tracy, born Jan. 5, 1722. The above Francis Tracy, Sen., died Nov. 28, 1755.

Mary Tracy and Benjamin Parrish were married April 18, 1705.

Jerusha Tracy and Thomas Rix were married June 26, 1718.

Christopher Tracy and Lydia Parrish were married May 20, 1705. Their children were: Lydia Tracy, born May 5, 1706; Mary Tracy, born Jan. 14, 1708, died June 25, 1708; Hannah Tracy, born April 27, 1709; Christopher Tracy, born June 1, 1711; Jonathan Tracy, born Dec. 16, 1713; Lidsay Tracy, born Feb. 9, 1716; Bethia Tracy, born July 19, 1718; Dorothy Tracy, born Jan. 11, 1720; Esther Tracy, born Jan. 19, 1721; Deborah Tracy, born April 29, 1722; Jerusha Tracy, born May 4, 1723; Solomon Tracy, born Aug. 8, 1724. The above named Christopher Tracy died Feb. 9, 1725.

Abigail Tracy and Benjamin Freeman were married Jan. 2, 1775.

Ziporah Tracy and Charles Freeman were married April 14, 1737.

Deborah Tracy and Elisha Adams were married November 9, 1720.

Jedediah Tracy's children were: Nathan Tracy, born Feb. 21, 1729; Benjamin Tracy died Sept. 8, 1731; Simon Tracy, born May 17, 1732; Ezra Tracy, born Oct. 15, 1734; Temperence Tracy, born Aug. 9, 1737.

David Tracy and Sarah Parrish were married Oct. 6, 1709. Their children were: Sarah Tracy, born June 17, 1710; Mary Tracy, born April 2, 1712, died March 31, 1715; Zerniah Tracy, born Sept. 12, 1714; Ziporah Tracy, born Sept. 19, 1716; Mary Tracy, born Nov. 25, 1718; David Tracy, born May 7, 1721; Lemuel Tracy, born Nov. 25, 1722; Rachael Tracy, born Nov. 29, 1724; Irene Tracy, born Jan. 19, 1726. Sarah Tracy, wife of the above David Tracy, died Jan. 10, 1729.

Nathaniel Tracy and Sarah Minor were married May 21, 1703. Their children were: Nathaniel Tracy, born March 15, 1707; Daniel Tracy, born Jan. 18, 1709; Beniah Tracy, born July 21, 1710; Joseph Tracy, born April 2, 1712.

Thomas Tracy's children: Nathaniel Tracy, born Dec. 19, 1675; Sarah Tracy, born Dec. 17, 1677; Jeremiah Tracy, born Oct. 14, 1682; Daniel Tracy, born March 3, 1685; Thomas Tracy, born June 15, 1687; Jedediah Tracy, born Sept. 24, 1692; Deborah and Jerusha Tracy, born Sept. 24, 1697.

Daniel Tracy died March 2, 1704.

Jedediah Tracy, of Preston, and Jerusha Richards of Norwich, were married March 29, 1739. Their children were: Jedediah Tracy, born May 12, 1740; Asahel Tracy, born Aug. 11, 1744; Jerusha Tracy, born May 26, 1747; Rufus Tracy, born May 30, 1749; Margaret Tracy, born Nov. 15, 1751.

Christopher Tracy and Elizabeth Tyler, both of Preston, were married March 26, 1781. Their children were: Ruth Tracy born May 18, 1724; Desire Tracy, born March 10, 1735; Christopher Tracy, born Dec. 8, 1737; Anne Tracy, born Nov. 16, 1739; Jonathan Tracy, born April 29, 1742. Christopher Tracy died Nov. 15, 1743.

Samuel Tracy and Esther Richmond were married Sept. 26, 1723. Their children were: Samuel Tracy, born Oct. 12, 1724; Esther Tracy, born Sept. 19, 1735, died Jan. 10, 1736; second Esther Tracy, born Feb. 25, 1738; Prisilla Tracy, born May 29, 1740; Elizabeth Tracy, born April 28, 1743; Miriam Tracy, born May 20, 1745; Stephen Tracy, born Nov. 12, 1748; Lucretia Tracy born Jan. 21, 1750.

Benajah Tracy, of Preston, and Hannah Safford, of Norwich, were married Dec. 25, 1735. Their children were: Sarah Tracy, born Nov. 14, 1736; Benajah Tracy, born Nov. 18, 1738, died Aug. 10, 1741; Hannah Tracy, born March 17, 1742.

Rebeckah Tracy, daughter of Jonathan Tracy and Amee, his wife, was born Sept. 12, 1726; Moses Tracy, born April 3, 1728; Samuel Tracy, born Feb. 28, 1731; Anna Tracy, born April 1, 1733; Amee Tracy, born Nov. 12, 1735; Lois Tracy, born Nov. 2, 1737, died May 2, 1739; Dorothy Tracy, born March 28, 1740, died April 6, 1740; Jonathan Tracy, born April 11, 1741; Perez Tracy, born June 18, 1744. Amee, wife of said Jonathan Tracy, died Oct. 13, 1744.

Lydia Tracy and Adam Parke were married May 18, 1732.

Enoch Tracy, son of Thomas Tracy and Abigail, his wife, was born April 15, 1736; Phebe Tracy, born May 21, 1738, died March 15, 1739; Deborah Tracy, born Jan. 20, 1740; Elijah Tracy, born July 21, 1741; Sarah Tracy, born May 24, 1743. Mr. Thomas Tracy died Feb. 23, 1755.

Francis Tracy and Esther Rude, both of Preston, were married July 31, 1740. Their children were: Sarah Tracy, born April 15, 1741; John Tracy, born July 11, 1743; Seth Tracy, born March 13, 1747, died Nov. 15, 1748; Elisha Tracy, born Aug. 21, 1749; Huldah Tracy, born March 18, 1752; Lucy Tracy, born Aug. 7, 1754; Kezia Tracy born July 28, 1757; Silas

Tracy, born July 17, 1759. The above Kezia Tracy died March 17, 1761.

Benjamin Tracy, son of Jedediah Tracy and Mercy, his wife, was born in Preston, Aug. 2, 1742. Mrs. Mercy Tracy, the wife of Deacon Jedediah Tracy, died May 24, 1775. Deacon Jedediah Tracy died June 8, 1779, in the 87th year of his age.

Esther Tracy and Ebenezer Bennett, both of Preston, were married Oct. 28, 1742.

Zerniah Tracy and Joseph Branch were married Jan. 27, 1781.

Sheribiah Tracy and Mr. Wenworth, both of Preston, were married May 22, 1746.

Jonathan Tracy, of Preston, and Lucy Avery, of Norwich, were married May 19, 1747.

Children of Christopher Tracy and Elizabeth, his wife, were: Elizabeth Tracy, born Jan. 14, 1744; Lydia Tracy, born Dec. 6, 1745; Solomon Tracy, born Feb. 11, 1748, died Sept. 12, 1750; Ziporah Tracy, born 12, 1754. Elizabeth Tracy, the wife of Christopher Tracy, died Sept. 11, 1757. Christopher Tracy and Rose Tracy, both of Preston, were married March 22, 1758.

Richmond Tracy, son of Samuel and Esther Tracy, was born Sept. 9, 1753. Samuel Tracy, son of Samuel and Esther Tracy, died at Fort Edward, Nov. 27, 1756.

Isaac Tracy and Mehetible Rude, both of Preston, were married July 13, 1742. Their children were: Isaac Tracy, born April 10, 1743; Mary Tracy, born Feb. 17, 1745; Ziporah Tracy born Jan. 30, 1748; Zanan Tracy, born April 1, 1750; Bathsheba Tracy, born April 27, 1752; Mehetible Tracy, born May 13, 1754; Solomon Tracy, born June 1, 1756; Louise Tracy, born June 4, 1758; Zemrah Tracy, born Oct. 16, 1760; Keturah Tracy, born at Delaware, Feb. 28, 1763; Thankful Tracy, born April 25, 1765; Betsey Tracy, born Jan. 26, 1768.

Benajah Tracy and Lucy Herrick, both of Preston, were married July 1, 1762. Their children were: Elias Tracy, born April 5, 1763; Elisha Tracy, born Aug. 9, 1764; Robert Tracy, born Oct. 23, 1765; Hannah Tracy, born Aug. 9, 1767; Safford Tracy, born Nov. 4. 1768; Barten Tracy, born June 12, 1773; Elizabeth Tracy, born May 4, 1776; Lucy Tracy, born Oct. 28, 1778; Luther Tracy, born Oct. 21, 1780.

Levi Tracy, son of Jedediah and Jerusha Tracy, was born June 5, 1754; Sabra Tracy, born June 30, 1756; Eunice Tracy, born Aug. 30, 1758; Jedediah Tracy, born April 5, 1761. Mr. Jedediah Tracy, Jr., departed this life Jan. 26, 1766.

Ruth Tracy, daughter of Thomas Tracy and wife, was born Feb. 14, 1757.

Moses Tracy and Esther Tracy, both of Preston, were married June 4, 1755. Their children were: Edward Tracy, born July 7, 1756; Anna Tracy, born Sept. 25, 1762. Their son Samuel died March 5, 1764.

Ruth Tracy and Samuel Rennals, both of Preston, were married Feb. 26, 1756.

Daniel Tracy, of Preston, and Mary Kennedy, of Norwich, were married April 10, 1755. Their children were: Solomon Tracy, born March 1, 1756; Lemuel Tracy, born March 16, 1758; Rachel Tracy, born Aug. 5, 1759; second Lemuel Tracy, born Aug. 12, 1761.

Samuel Tracy, Jr., and Anna Partridge, both of Preston, were married May 15, 1755. Their children were: Elijah Tracy, born April 26, 1756; Cyrus Tracy, born Aug. 6, 1757; Eunice Tracy, born Dec. 2, 1758; Bela Tracy, born April 3, 1761; Diana Tracy, born Feb. 15, 1763; Jonathan Tracy, born Nov. 1, 1764; Deborah Tracy, born Sept. 12, 1766; Samuel P. Tracy, born March 21, 1769; Lucy Tracy, born Feb. 6, 1771; Amy Tracy, born Sept. 11, 1774.

Prisilla Tracy and John Branch, Jr., both of Preston, were married Jan. 5, 1758.

Simeon Tracy and Lois Branch, both of Preston, were married Sept. 13, 1758. Their children were: Seth Tracy, born Oct. 18, 1759; Elem Tracy, born Aug. 3, 1761; Mercy Tracy, born Sept. 6, 1763; Aseniah Tracy, born June 30, 1766.

John Tracy and H.....h Haskell, both of Norwich, were married Jan. 28, 1755. ....athaniel Tracy, their son, was born Sept. 12, 1757.

Ezra Tracy, of Preston, and Jemima K..nball, of Stonington, were married Jan. 24, 1760. Their children were: Gilbert Tracy. born Jan. 7, 1761; Sanford Tracy, born July 20, 1762; Wealthy Tracy, born March 17, 1765; Elisha Tracy, born Sept. 30, 1768; Erastus Tracy, born Feb, 20, 1771; Anne Tracy, born Feb. 22, 1773; Margret Tracy, born Aug. 13, 1775: Appleton Tracy. born Feb. 2.0, 1779; Jedediah Tracy, born Aug. 14, 17..).

Sarah Tracy, of Norwich, and John Cook, Jr., of Preston, were married Nov. 11, 1755.

Thankful Tracy and Nathan Rude, both of Preston. were married April 30, 17.1.

Hannah Tracy and Barton Cook, both of Preston, were maried Oct. 14, 1762.

Temperance Tracy and Nathan Forbes, both of Preston, were married May 5, 1763. Mrs. Tempei..nce Forbes died Dec. 8, 18.7, in the 70th year of her age.

Benjamin Tracy and Olive Kil...m, both of P..ston, were married Nov. 17, 1763. Their children were: Lucy Tracy, born May 18, 1765; Avery Tracy, born June 26, 1767; John Tracy, born Jan. 27, 1770; Shubael Tracy, born Feb. 12. 1773; Mercy Tracy, born Sept. 16, 17.5; Ab..ga.. Tracy, born Feb. 17, 1778; Betsy Tracy, born April 26, 17..).

Olive Tracy, of Norwich, and Daniel Wit..r, of Preston, were married July 16, 1769.

Asahel Tracy and Olive Le.....rd, both of Preston, were m.. ..ried Feb. 16, 1769. Th..i.. c..ldren were: Rufus Tracy, born Dec. 9, 1769; William T..., born Jan. 23, 1771, died Nov. 15, 1772; Robert Tracy, born March 27, 1773; Mary Tracy, born March 27, 1775; W..liam Tracy, bo..n Dec. 7, 1776; Clarissa Tracy, born March 10, 1779; Sabra Tracy, born Oct. 22, 1780; Olive Tracy, born Jan. 22, 17.. .. Mr. Asahel Tracy, died Feb. 21, 18..2.

Jabez Tracy, of Preston, and Prudence Fanning, of Groton, were married April 25, 1770. Chester Tracy, their son, was born Sept. 12, 1771.

Jerusha Tracy and Nathan Geer, both of Preston, were married May 1, 1766.

Rufus Tracy, of Preston, and Mary Reed, of Norwich, were married April 9, 1775.

Ruth Tracy, of Norwich, and Israel Herrick, of Preston, were married Jan. 5, 1775.

————o————

Of John Tracy, the third, who married Margaret Hyde. They settled at Norwich, West Farms, now Franklin, where he died August, 1783. She died Feb. 6, 1789, at Franklin. Their children were: John, born Feb. 11, 1726, at Norwich, married first, Margaret Huntington, second, Bethia Johnson; Eleazer, born March 16, 1728, at Norwich, who left his paternal home when young and unmarried, and was never afterwards heard of by his relatives. Supposed to have been killed in the French war; Josiah, born April 17, 1720, at Norwich, married Margaret Pettis; Hezekiah, born in 1726, at Norwich, married first, Elizabeth Pettis, second, Abigail Starr; Daniel, born March 14, 1728, at Norwich, married Mary Johnson; Theophilus, born Sept. 14, 1742, at Norwich, married Sarah Gifford; Joshua, born Aug. 13, 1745, at Norwich, married Naoma Bingham; Elizabeth, born May 1, 1732, at Norwich, married Zebulon Edgerton; Margaret, born May 16, 1734, at Norwich, married William Bentley; Rachel, born Sept. 27, 1740, at Norwich, married Dec. 6, 1768, her second cousin, Ezekiel Hyde, second son of Jabez Hyde, the second, and Lydia Abel, of Norwich.

Esther Hyde, born at Norwich, Conn., Feb. 16, 1709, the third daughter of John Hyde and Experience Abel, was a granddaughter of Samuel Hyde, the first, and Jane Lee, of Norwich.

She married, Feb. 5, 1740, Thomas Williams. I suppose he was of the Montville family, and that he was a son of Thomas Williams, who died 1705. He died March 23, 1746, at Norwich, and she died April 29, 1799, at Franklin. Their children were: Thomas, born March 22, 1742, at Norwich, married Jerusha Abel; Esther, born May 30, 1740, at Norwich, who I have not been able to trace further; Ruth, born Jan. 19, 1744, at Norwich died Dec. 16, 1798, at Franklin, unmarried.

Lucy Hyde, born at Norwich, Conn., April 16, 1713, the fourth daughter of John Hyde and Experience Abel, was a granddaughter of Samuel Hyde, the first, and Jane Lee, of Norwich. She married, Nov, 25, 1733, Asa Waterman, born Nov. 15, 1706, at Norwich, the youngest son of Ensign Thomas Waterman, the second, and Elizabeth Allyn, of Norwich. This Ensign Thomas Waterman, was the eldest son of Ensign Thomas Waterman, one of the original proprietors of Norwich, who was born in 1644 at Marshfield, son of Robert Waterman and Elizabeth Bourn. He married, Nov. 1668, Miriam Tracy, the only daughter of Lt. Thomas Tracy, of Norwich, and died in 1708. He had by her three sons and five daughters: Thomas, who married, June 29, 1691, Elizabeth Allyn; John, who married first, Nov. 5, 1701, Elizabeth Lathrop, second, Sept. 27, 1709, Mrs. Judith Woodward, third, April 16, 1721, Elizabeth Bassett; Joseph, who married Elizabeth Woodward; Elizabeth, who married July 10, 1695, Capt. John Fitch, of Windham; Miriam, who died Sept. 22, 1760, unmarried, Martha, who married June 30, 1709, and was the second wife of "Lyme's Captain," Deacon Reynold Marvin, of Lyme; Lydia, who married Nov. 25, 1708, Eleazer Burnam; Anne, who married Nov. 4, 1713, Josiah de Wolf, of Lyme.

The children of Thomas Waterman, second, and Elizabeth Allyn, were: Thomas, born 1692; John, born 1694; Elizabeth, born 1696; Ebenezer, born 1699; Daniel, born 1701; Elisha, born 1704; Asa, born 1706; and probably Sarah and Nehemiah.

John Waterman, the first, by his three wives, had eleven

children: Elizabeth, born 1702; Eleazer, born 1704; John, born 1706, died 1730, unmarried; Hannah, born 1708; William, born 1710; Samuel, born 1712; Ebenezer, born 1715; Peter, born 1717; Mary, born 1722; David B., born 1725; Elizabeth, born 1730.

Joseph Waterman and Elizabeth Woodward, had seven children: Timothy, born 1717; Judith, born 1720; Ezra, born 1725; Elizabeth, born 1724; Mehetible, born 1727; Anne, born 1730; Joseph, born 1733, died 1753.

Asa Waterman and his wife, Lucy Hyde, settled at Norwich, where he died Nov. 14, 1783. She survived him, and died there, Nov. 16, 1790. Their children were: Thomas, born Aug. 12, 1734, at Norwich, married Eunice French; Asa, born May 1, 1743, at Norwich, married Anne Sterry; Azariah, born Dec. 18, 1745, died Sept. 7, 1753; Aruna, born April 24, 1749, at Norwich, married Hannah Leffingwell; second Azariah, born Oct. 1, 1754, died Sept. 5, 1759; Lucy, born Jan. 15, 1757, at Norwich, married her second cousin, Judge Matthew Adgate, the fourth son of Hannah Hyde and Matthew Adgate; Mary, born April 19, 1759, at Norwich, married her second cousin, Capt. Jedediah Hyde, the eldest son of the Rev. Jedediah Hyde, by his first wife Jerusha Perkins; Deborah, born May 8, 1741, died June 2, 1755,

Lois Gifford, born at Norwich, Conn., Feb. 25, 1731, the third daughter of Samuel Gifford and Experience Hyde, of Norwich, was a grand-daughter of John Hyde, of the third generation. She married Jan. 3, 1753, Theophilus Huntington, born Sept. 12, 1726, son of Christopher Huntington, of Norwich, by his first wife, Abigail Abel-Lathrop. They settled at Norwich. He was clerk of the Bozrah church from 1764 to 1778. In 1780 they removed to Lebanon, N. H., where he died in 1815. The date of her death I have not ascertained. Their children were: Theopilus, born Nov. 23, 1753, at Norwich, married, first, Ruth Talcott, second, Phebe Hall; Samuel, born July 29, 1755, at Norwich, married Mary Bennet; Hiram, born Aug. 24, 1758, at Norwich, married Lucy Perkins. Zika, born Oct. 26, 1760, at

Norwich, married Sila Green; Abel, born Dec. 2, 1762, at Norwich, died Sept. 9, 1778; Uriel, born May 7, 1771, at Norwich, married Elizabeth Hough; Nehemiah, born April 20, 1776, at Norwich, married Hannah N. Lathrop; Lois, born May 11, 1765, at Norwich, married May 15, 1783, Samuel Lathrop, of Lebanon, N. H., where she died April 4, 1849. He was a son of Elisha Lathrop, by his second wife, Hannah Hough; Margaret, born Nov. 2, 1768, at Norwich, married Rufus Lathrop, and lived at Chelsea, Vt., and left a family, the particulars of whom I have not fully ascertained.

Experience Gifford, born at Norwich, Conn., May 15, 1733, the fourth daughter of Samuel Gifford and Experience Hyde, of Norwich, was a grand-daughter of John Hyde, of the third generation. She married June 26, 1754, Isaac Johnson, born May 24, 1728, at Norwich, son of Ebenezer Johnson and Deborah Champion, of Norwich. They settled at Norwich, where she died May 7, 1755. His only child by her was Oliver, born May 5, 1755, at Norwich, married Martha Perkins. He then married, March 13, 1760, Jerusha Gager, born March 30, 1735, at Norwich, daughter of John Gager and Jerusha Barstow, and had by her a daughter, Jerusha, born Jan. 14, 1761, who married June 30, 1785, Dr. Elijah Hartshorn, of Norwich. Isaac Johnson's second wife died March 10, 1809, and he died Nov. 15, 1814, at Franklin.

John Tracy, born at Norwich, Conn., Feb. 11, 1726, the eldest son of John Tracy and Margaret Hyde, of Norwich, was a grand-son of John Hyde, of the third generation. He married Oct. 13, 1747, his third cousin, Margaret Huntington, born Nov. 23, 1724, at Norwich, daughter of Christopher Huntington and Abigail Abel-Lathrop, the widow of Barnabas Lathrop, of Norwich. They settled at Norwich, West Farms, (now Franklin,) where she died Dec. 23, 1755. He was a farmer. His children by her were: John, born Dec. 21, 1749, at Norwich, married Esther Pride; Mary, born April 1, 1750, at Norwich, married her father's second cousin, Andrew Hyde, the third son of Jabez

Hyde and Lydia Abel, of Norwich; Margaret, born May 29, 1753 at Norwich, married, first, Zebediah Lathrop, second, Benjamin Storrs; Lydia, born 1755, died young and unmarried. After the death of his first wife, he married Jan. 19, 1758, Bethia Johnson, born April 15, 1724, at Norwich, daughter of Ebenezer Johnson and Deborah Champion, of Norwich. She died Dec. 13, 1803. He survived her and died March 28, 1810, at Franklin. His children by her were: Eleazer, born April 28, 1759, at Norwich, died July 7, 1759; second Eleazer, born June 23, 1769, at Norwich, died Oct. 7, 1760; Oliver, born Jan. 11, 1769, at Norwich, married Lydia Rude; Erastus, born Feb. 11, 1771, at Norwich, married Clara Prentiss; Bethia, born April 14, 1764, at Norwich, died Sept. 9, 1764.

Josiah Tracy, born at Norwich, Conn., April 17, 1730, the third son of John Tracy and Margaret Hyde, of Norwich, was a grand-son of John Hyne, of the third generation. He married Dec. 15, 1757, Margaret Pettis, born March 4, 1740, daughter of Peter Pettis and Abigail Failes, of Norwich. He was a farmer, and they settled at Norwich, West Farms, (now Franklin.) He died Jan. 24, 1806. She survived him, and died Sept. 6, 1821. Their children were: Eleazer, born March 21, 1764, at Norwich, married first, Prudee Bogers, second, widow Hannah Tracy; Peter, born April 19, 1767, at Norwich, married Abigail Hartshorn; Josiah, born May 7, 1772, at Norwich, married Mary Birchard; Zebediah, born July 18, 1782, at Norwich, died Aug. 15, 1783; Cynthia, born Sept. 6, 1758, at Norwich, married her second cousin, Joshua Hyde, the eldest son of Silas Hyde and Martha Waterman, of Norwich; Lucy, born Oct. 7, 1760, at Norwich, married Daniel Tracy; Margaret, born Dec. 14, 1762, at Norwich, married her second cousin, Abel Hyde, the second son of Silas Hyde and Martha Waterman, of Norwich; Bethia, born July 16, 1769, at Norwich, married Andrew Veach Williams, of Lebanon, son of Veach Williams and Lucy Walworth, of Lebanon, and had one son, Veach born April 17, 1797, who died in childhood. Her husband died Oct. 12, 1828, at Lebanon. She died Feb. 28, 1848. at Mohegan ; Lucretia, born Sept. 4, 1774, at Norwich, married William Bailey ; Rachel, born March 6, 1777, at Norwich, married Cyrenus Clark ; Naoma, born May 17, 1780, at Norwich, married Joseph H. Willes.

Lieut. Hezekiah Tracy, born at Norwich, Conn., in 1736, the fourth son of John Tracy and Margaret Hyde, of Norwich, was a grand-son of John Hyde, of the third generation. He married Aug. 9, 1759, Elizabeth Pettis, born Dec. 29. 1737, at Norwich, the eldest daughter of Joshua Pettis, of Norwich, by his first wife, Elizabeth Crocker. They settled at Norwich, where she died, Nov. 9, 1791. He afterwards married the widow Abigail Starr, but had no issue by her. He died June 23, 1817, at Franklin, aged 81. His children were : Dudley, born Sept. 28, 1700, at Norwich, married Sarah Kingsbury ; Joshua, born Oct. 16, 1768; at Norwich, married first, Sarah Paine, second, the widow Martha Hastings ; Hezekiah, born May 5, 1771, at Norwich, married Eunice Packard, of Albany, and settled at Greenwich, Conn. She died May 26, 1801. He died July 10, 1829. They had two children : Eliza, born June 17, 1798, died Oct. 17, 1799, and John Jay, born July 2, 1800; Elizabeth, born Dec. 1, 1762, at Norwich, died unmarried ; Wealthy, born Feb. 13, 1767, at Norwich died unmarried.

Daniel Tracy, born at Norwich, Conn., March 14, 1738, the fifth son of John Tracy and Margaret Hyde, of Norwich, was a grand-son of John Hyde, of the third generation. He married Sept. 16, 1702, Mary Johnson, born April 7, 1738, at Norwich, daughter of Ebenezer Johnson and Deborah Champion, of Norwich. They settled at Norwich, where they probably both died, but I have not ascertained the dates of their deaths. Their children were : Uri, born Feb. 8, 1764. at Norwich, married Ruth Hovey ; Hiel, born July 5, 1766, at Norwich, married Susannah Gifford ; James, born Feb. 9, 1770, at Norwich, married first, Ruth Calkins, second, Margoret Wheeler ; Daniel, born Aug. 3, 1774, at Norwich, married Mary Havens ; Mary, born Sept. 22, 1772, at Norwich, married Daniel Baldwin, of Chenango county, and had two daughters: Mary, who married Pardon Smith, of Oxford, and ———, who married ——— Corbin, of McDonough, New York.

Theophilus Tracy, born at Norwich, Conn., Sept. 14, 1742, the sixth son of John Tracy and Margaret Hyde, of Norwich, was a grand-son of John Hyde, of the third generation. He married Dec. 10, 1766, his first cousin, Sarah Gifford, born June 22, 1744, at Norwich, the youngest daughter of Samuel Gifford and Experience Hyde, of Norwich. He was a farmer, and they settled at Norwich, West Farms, (now Franklin.) They subsequently removed to Granville, N. Y., where he died in 1812. She survived him and removed to Hartwick, N. Y. Their children were: Theophilus, born Nov. 16, 1768, at Norwich, married Thankful Draper; Riel, born Dec. 5, 1774, at Norwich, married Dimis Anne Martin; Stephen, born Nov. 4, 1776, at Norwich, married widow Wade; Sarah, born Dec. 15, 1770, at Norwich, married March 11, 1793, Dr. William Livingston, of Salem, N. Y., and removed to St. Lawrence county; Experience, born Dec. 16, 1772, at Norwich, died May 16, 1793, at Granville, unmarried; Wealthy, born Oct. 2, 1778, at Norwich, married Sylvanus West; Anna, born Oct. 6, 1780, at Norwich, died May 4, 1796, unmarried; Hannah, born June 20, 1783, at Norwich, married William Loring, of Spencer, N. Y.; Ruth, born May 16, 1785, at Norwich; Lura, born May 11, 1788, at Franklin, married Prince West.

Lieut. Joshua Tracy, born at Norwich, Conn., August 13, 1745, the seventh son of John Tracy and Margaret Hyde, of Norwich, was a grand-son of John Hyde of the third generation. He married May 22, 1771, Naoma Bingham, of Windham, born May 13, 1744, daughter of Jonathan Bingham and Mary Abbe, of Windham, and grand-daughter of John Abbe, the first, of Wenham, Mass. He died March 20, 1777, at Norwich, of the small-pox, and was burried on the hill in Franklin, near Dr. Woodward's. Their children were: Abel, born April 26, 1772, at Norwich. I have not been able to get any further account of him, and presume he must have died s. p, ; Thomas, born May 23, 1774, at Norwich; Joshua, born Dec. 21, 1776, at Norwich, died Aug. 11, 1779.

Elizabeth Tracy, born at Norwich, Conn., May 1, 1732, the eldest daughter of John Tracy and Margaret Hyde, was a grand-daughter of John Hyde, of the third generation. She married July 9, 1753, Zebulon Edgerton, born Nov. 14, 1728, at Norwich, son of Samuel Edgerton and Margaret Abel, her third cousin. They settled at Norwich, West Farms, (now Franklin) where he died Feb. 6, 1796. She survived him, and died Oct. 5, 1821, at Franklin, aged 89 years. Their children were: Zebulon, born March 4, 1754, at Norwich, married Abigail ———; John, born May 18, 1768, at Norwich, died Oct. 27, 1778: Elizabeth, born Dec. 14, 1755. at Norwich, she probably married her first cousin, Eleazer Bentley, son of William Bentley and Margaret Tracy; Margaret, born April 10, 1758, at Norwich; Silence, born March 1. 1760, at Norwich; Anne J., born Nov. 7, 1762, at Norwich, probably married Jan. 21, 1787, at Franklin, Ezra Edgerton, born Jan. 17, 1752, third son of William Edgerton and Lydia Barstow; Bethia, born Sept. 8, 1764, at Norwich, probably married Elephelet Metcalf; Rachel, born June 12, 1770, at Norwich, she probably married Jan. 24, 1791, Jehial Root, at Franklin; Asenath, born Aug. 80, 1772, at Norwich. She lived at Franklin, where she died Oct. 23, 1836, unmarried.

Margaret Tracy, born at Norwich, Conn., May 16, 1734, the second daughter of John Tracy and Margaret Hyde, of Norwich, was a grand-daughter of John Hyde, of the third generation. She married Aug. 5, 1755, William Bentley. They settled in that part of Norwich which is now Franklin, where they had one child recorded to them. That child was Eleazer, born at Norwich. He married Feb. 14, 1788, Elizabeth Edgerton, and settled at Franklin. They had one son and two daughters: Elizabeth, born May 19, 1793, at Franklin, married Oct. 23, 1829, Fidelia Henry, of Lebanon; Margaret, born Aug. 4, 1789, at

Franklin, died Nov. 7, 1812, unmarried; Bethia, born Dec. 24, 1791, at Franklin.

Thomas Williams, born at Norwich, March 23, 1742, son of Thomas Williams and Esther Hyde, of Norwich, was a grandson of John Hyde, of the third generation. He married Dec. 6, 1767, Jerusha Abel, born March 11, 1748, at Norwich, second daughter of John Abel and Hannah Gifford, of Norwich. They settled at Norwich, where they had one child recorded to them. That child was Elisha, born March 14, 1770, at Norwich.

Thomas Waterman, born at Norwich, Conn., Aug. 12, 1724, the eldest son of Asa Waterman and Lucy Hyde, of Norwich, was a grand-son of John Hyde, of the third generation. He married May 27, 1759, Eunice French, born July, 24, 1739, at Norwich, the second daughter of Samuel French and Elizabeth White, of Norwich. They settled at Norwich, where he was drowned in 1773, while washing sheep. Their children were: Azariah, born April 3, 1761, at Norwich. He was a soldier in the army of the revolution, and was on board the Jersey prison ship. Upon his exchange he took the small-pox, of which he died soon after his return home, unmarried; Erastus, born March 19, 1773, at Norwich. He lived at Norwich, and died March 16, 1850, unmarried; Lucy, born Sept. 22, 1763, at Norwich. She married ——— Bostwich and settled at Charleton, N. Y., and had seven children: Elizabeth Maria, Sarah Anne, Lucy, Harriet, Rhoda Thompson, Olive Eliza, and a son, who was a purser in the U. S. navy, and was lost at sea; Eunice, born Jan. 15, 1765, at Norwich. She married Nov. 24, 1791, Abner Backus, Esq., born Oct. 10, 1767, at Norwich. They settled at Norwich, where he was a landholder. He died May 30, 1845, and she died Sept. 9, 1816, sine prole; Caroline, born March 25, 1769, at Norwich. She married ——— Barlow, and probably removed to Saratoga county, N. Y., and had several children, one of whom was Samuel.

John Tracy, born at Norwich, Conn., Dec. 21, 1755, eldest son of John Tracy of Norwich, by his first wife, Margaret Huntington, was a great grand-son of John Hyde, of the third generation. He married May 24, 1780, Esther Pride, of Lisbon. They settled in that part of Norwich which is now Franklin. In 1806 they removed to Columbus, N. Y., where he died Jan. 14, 1821. She died in June, 1838. Their children were: John, born Oct. 26, 1783, at Norwich, married Aug. 5, 1813, his father's third cousin, Susannah Hyde, born July 3, 1787, at Franklin, second daughter of Joseph Hyde, and Susannah Waterman. He was a lawyer, and they settled at Oxford, N. Y., where he was a member of the Legislature. He was lieutenant-governor of the state for six years, and was president of the constitutional convention of 1846. They were living in Oxford in 1862. They had three children, born at Oxford: John, born June 20, 1820, died Dec. 24, 1820. He was the seventh John in descent from Lieut. Thomas Tracy, the first, of Norwich, who came from England, the eldest son of each generation being named John Tracy: Esther Maria, born April 9, 1816, married Dec. 2, 1835, Henry Rowland Mygatt, born April 10, 1810, eldest son of Henry Mygatt and Sarah S. Washburn, of Oxford, grand-son of Noadiah Mygatt and Clarissa Lynde, of New Milford, and was the eighth in descent from Joseph Mygatt, born in England in 1596, who came to Newtown, Mass., in the Griffin, in 1633, with his wife Anne, and settled at Hartford in 1636, (see Mygatt Genealogy.) Henry Rowland Mygatt graduated at Union College in 1830, and was a lawyer. They settled at Oxford, where they were living in 1858. They had two children: John Tracy, born Nov. 29, 1836, who graduated at Union College in 1858, and in 1861, married Sarah Dickinson, daughter of D. S. Dickinson; William Roland, born April 10, 1851: Susan Eliza, born April 9, 1816, (twin of Esther Maria,) She was living with her parents in 1860, unmarried; Zebediah Lathrop, born Oct. 8, 1783, at Franklin, married Dorothy Robinson, of Danbury, Conn., and settled at Durhamville, N. Y., where she died. He had by her three children: Fayette, born August, 1818; Frederick W., born May 28, 1820, and Harriet. He then married Frances Hibbard, and died Jan. 6, 1852.

He had by her a daughter, Susan Melissa; Ulysses, born Aug. 13, 1790, at Franklin, died July 28, 1791; Bela, born April 19, 1794, at Franklin, married Carlista Spurr, of Columbus, N. Y., and removed to Sinclairville, in Charlotte, N. Y. They had six children: Emely, born Oct. 23, 1826; Pamelia, born Aug. 27, 1828; Melissa, born May 7, 1830; John, born Feb. 10, 1832; Austin, born June 1, 1834; Lewis, born July 2, 1842; second Ulysses, born Jan. 4, 1833, at Franklin, married October, 1835, Jane L. Bunker, of the city of New York, and in 1838, removed to Chautauque county, where he died Aug. 19, 1840 They had two children: Esther and Henry; Rachel, born Aug. 22, 1781, at Norwich, married Andrew Palmer, of Mansfield, Conn. She died Oct. 29, 1852, in Wisconsin. They had four children, and perhaps more: John, Nelson, Emeline and Catherine; Harriet, born May 16, 1792, at Franklin, married Oct. 3, 1811, at Columbus, N. Y., Otis Eddy, born Jan. 20, 1787, in Rhode Island, son of Willard Eddy and Dorcas Matthewson. (This Willard Eddy was born Jan. 21, 1760, in Rhode Island, and about 1795, removed to Richfield, N. Y., where he died April 13, 1854, at the advanced age of 94 years. He was a son of Enoch Eddy, grand son of Zachariah Eddy, great grand-son of John Edddy, great great grand-son of John Eddy, and great great great grand-son of Samuel Eddy, who was born in England, and came to Plymouth, Mass., in 1630, in the ship Handmaid, of which John Grant was master.) Otis Eddy was a carpenter, manufacturer, and a canal constructor. They settled at New Berlin, N. Y., and afterwards removed to Ithaca, where he was a mill owner. He died Sept. 5, 1813, at Sinclairville, in the town of Charlotte, N. Y., while on a visit to his brother-in-law. She was living at Brooklyn, N. Y., in 1858, with her youngest son. They had six children: the two first born at New Berlin, and the others at Ithaca. Willard Tracy, born Sept. 13, 1812, married July 17, 1836, his first cousin, Susan Williams, born July 6, 1819, eldest daughter of James Williams and Esther Tracy, of Gerry, N. Y. They were living at Fredonia, N. Y., in 1858, and had three children: Harriet Emily, born Sept. 30, 1838; Susan Maria, born Oct. 20, 1845, and Willard Tracy, born June 20, 1849. Lathrop Storrs, born July 1, 1814, married June, 1839, Adeline E. Hargin, of Ithaca, N. Y. He was a lawyer, and practiced his profession for some years in the state of New York, and was an examiner in chancery. He went to California, and died Nov. 9, 1851, at sea, on his return passage from San Francisco to Panama. She died March, 1852, at Ithaca. They had one child: Lathrop Storrs, born Sept. 1, 1844. Axala Fayette, born Oct. 18, 1816, at Ithaca, and died Oct. 1, 1817, at Ithaca; William Matthewson, born Aug. 16, 1818, married May 8, 1844, at Portsmouth, R. I., Hannah Anthony, daughter of David Anthony, of Portsmouth. He was a civil engineer, and she died in 1847, at New York, s. p. He then went to San Francisco, Cal., and was surveyor-general of that state. He again married in 1851, at San Francisco, Harriet Eacker, formerly of Ithaca. He died March 9, 1854, at San Francisco, where she was living in 1858, He had by her one child: Charles Eacker, born in 1853; James, born Oct. 23, 1821, at Ithaca, married May 7, 1844, Maria Judd, born May 26, 1824, at Ithaca, daughter of Reuben Judd and Minerva Stevens, of Ithaca, who were married May 4, 1814, at Williamstown, Mass. James Eddy and wife, resided at Portsmouth, R. I., Ithaca, N. Y., Bangor and Portland, Me. In 1855 they removed to Brooklyn, N. Y., where they were living in 1858. He was the general superintendent of the American telegraph company. They had two children: Otis Judd, born June 30, 1846, at Ithaca; and Charles, born Feb. 28, 1850, at Bangor; Harriet Emely, born Oct. 3, 1826, at Ithaca, where she died Dec. 6, 1826; Esther, born Nov. 8, 1793, at Franklin, married April 16, 1817, at Columbus, N. Y., James Williams, born Sept. 20, 1792, at Newport, R. I., son of Obadiah Williams and Dorcas Earl. He was a farmer, and they lived at various places in New York, New Jersey and Pennsylvania. In 1835 they removed to Gerry, N. Y., where they were living in 1858. They had nine children: Frederick Tracy, born Feb. 3, 1818, at head of Cayuga lake, married Oct. 24, 1841, at Ellery, N. Y., Anne H. Aldrich, youngest daughter of Tillson Aldrich and Sarah Metcalf. He was a farmer, and they settled at Ellery, where he died April 3, 1853, and where she was living in 1858. They had two children: Sarah Maria, born May 28, 1846, and Frederick Tillson, born Sept. 16, 1853; Susan, born June 9, 1819, at head of Cayuga lake, married July 17, 1836, her first cousin, William Tracy Eddy, eldest son of Otis Eddy and Harriet Tracy, of Ithaca; Emely, born Aug. 25, 1821, at Berks county, Pa., married Nov. 8, 1840, at Gerry, Josiah Fisher. He was a carpenter, and in 1858 they were living at Weyauwega, Wis. They had five children: Mary, born Sept. 23, 1844; Henry, born Oct. 21, 1846; Esther Ella, born Sept. 22, 1848; Jennie Maria, born Jan. 18, 1851; George William, born Nov. 13, 1854; Henry, born Aug. 12, 1823, in New Jersey, died Oct. 13, 1827; Maria, born April 2), 1825, at New York, died Nov. 5, 1827; Henry H., born Sept. 25, 1828, at Hudson. He was living at Ossawatamie, Kansas, in 1858, unmarried, where he was a colonel of militia, and a member of the legislature, and sheriff. He was an architect; second Maria, born Dec. 31, 1830, at Ithaca. married May 21, 1855, at Gerry, Lorenzo Somberger, second son of Henry Somberger and Chloe Holms. He was a farmer, and they were living at Gerry in 1858; George Tyler, born July 28, 1833, at Ithaca. He was a telegraph operator at Cleveland in 1858, unmarried; Edwin, born Sept. 19, 1837 at Gerry, where he was living in 1858, unmarried; Emely, born Nov. 10, 1798, at Franklin, married Dr. Hedges, a physician of Jamestown, N. Y., where she died Sept. 30, 1838, sine prole.

Margaret Tracy, born at Norwich, Conn., May 29, 1758, second daughter of John Tracy, of Norwich, by his first wife, Margaret Huntington, was a great grand-daughter of John Hyde, of the third generation. She married Sept. 22, 1783, Zebediah Lathrop, of Norwich, who died Oct. 4, 1783, s. p. She then married Sept. 14, 1785, Benjamin Storrs, of Mansfield, born May 21, 1752, fifth son of Huckins Stoors and Eunice Porter, of Mansfield. She had by him a family of children, but I have not been able to ascertain the particulars of that family, except the following children: Lathrop, Huckins, Oliver, Margaret·

Oliver Tracy, born at Norwich, Conn., Jan. 11, 1769, third son of John Tracy, of Norwich, by his second wife, Bethia Johnson, was a great grand-son of John Hyde, of the third generation. He married June 14, 1792, his fourth cousin, Lydia Rude, born about 1769, at Norwich, youngest daughter of Jonathan Rude and Talitha Ormsby. They settled at Franklin, where she died March 5, 1826, and he died May 8, 1846. Their children were: Samuel Rude, born July 10, 1795, at Franklin, died Oct. 7, 1796; Oliver, born Oct. 17, 1797, at Franklin. He was a farmer, and lived in Franklin, and was a member of the legislature. He died in 1858 at Franklin, unmarried; Almond, born Nov. 18, 1800, at Franklin, married Nov. 4, 1846, Abby Jane Huntington, born Nov. 15, 1825, daughter of his first cousin, Ziba Huntington and Abigail Ellis, of Franklin. They settled at Franklin at his father's homestead, where they were living in 1859. They had in 1856, three children: Oliver Rude, born Aug. 21, 1847; William John, born July 15, 1852, and Lydia Ellis, born Dec. 18, 1855; Lydia, born Oct. 8, 1793, at Franklin, died May 20, 1795.

Erastus Tracy, born at Norwich, Conn., Feb. 11, 1771, the youngest son of John Tracy, by his second wife, Bethia Johnson, was a great grand-son of John Hyde, of the third generation. He married Nov. 29, 1792, Clarissa Prentiss, of Franklin, born in 1772. They settled at Franklin, where he died March 1, 1832, and she died Dec. 11, 1838, aged 66 years. Their children were: Harley Hic, born Sept. 2, 1796, at Franklin, married Jan. 12, 1823, Mary Abel Bill, probably daughter of Phillip Bill and Hannah Abel, daughter of Simeon Abel and Martha Crocker. They settled at Franklin, and removed to Bozrah, where she died. He was living at Bozrah in 1859. They had seven children recorded at Franklin: Mary Louisa, born Jan. 26, 1824; Alice Abel, born March 29, 1827, married Oct. 16, 1849, her fourth cousin, John A, Maples, born March 7, 1826, fourth son of Capt. Joshua Maples and Elizabeth Rogers, of Bozrah; Erastus Philip, born

March 5, 1829; John, born May 8, 1831; Benjamin Franklin, born May 6, 1834; Hezekiah Abel, born Nov. 28, 1836, died Feb. 13, 1851; Elijah Abel, born Sept. 28, 1841, at Franklin. Charles Huntington, born Oct. 4, 1801, at Franklin, married Feb. 8, 1825, Almira Fargo, daughter of Gurdon Fargo, of Franklin. They settled at Franklin and had several children: Emely and Jane, both of whom married; Joseph, who died in infancy; and Noyes, a physician of Franklin. Clarissa, born Aug. 16, 1799, at Franklin, married Oct. 19, 1817, Uriah Hartshorn, son of Dr. Elijah Hartshorn and Jerusha Johnson, of Franklin. They settled and died at Franklin. They had in addition to some who died in childhood, three children: Mary; Henry, who married and settled at Darien or Pembroke, N. Y.; and Julia Frances.

Bethia Johnson, born Nov. 3, 1803, at Franklin, married April 1, 1827, Willard Gurdon Pember, born Feb. 5, 1805, at Franklin, eldest son of Thomas Pember and Theodosia Fillmore, of Franklin. They settled at Franklin, where she died April 15, 1829. He had by her one child: Bethia Tracy, born March 26, 1829, at Franklin, married Aug. 22, 1849, Lyman L. Apsley, of Canterbury.

Willard Gurdon Pember, after the death of his first wife, married Nov. 5, 1829, Frances A. Fargo, and was living at Franklin in 1859, and had by her seven other children: Julian Thomas born Oct. 2, 1830; Olivia Jennette, born Sept. 19, 1832, married March 13, 1853, John Benedick; John Luzerne, born Aug. 18, 1834; Williard Dwight, born Sept. 20, 1836; Lucius Gurdon, born March 30, 1841; Julia Frances, born Jan. 24, 1844; and Mary Etheridge, born Dec. 7, 1846, at Frandlin.

Major Eleazer Tracy, born at Norwich, Conn., March 21, 1764, eldest son of Josiah Tracy and Margaret Pettis, of Norwich, was a great grand-son of John Hyde, of the third generation. He married Sept. 14, 1788, his third cousin, Prudce Rogers, born July 8, 1766, at Norwich, third daughter of Capt. Uriah Rogers and Lydia Hyde, of Franklin, a great grand-daughter of Samuel Hyde, and also of William Hyde, of the third generation.

They settled at Franklin, where he was a man of very considerable consequence, and frequently represented the town in the state legislature. She died Nov. 22, 1813, at Franklin. He survived her, and married Hannah (Jones) Tracy, widow of his third cousin, Jabez Tracy, of Norwich. He died Feb. 25, 1841, at the residence of one of his daughters, at Mohegan, without issue by his second wife, and was burried at Franklin. His children by his first wife were: Eleazer, born Sept. 28, 1791, at Franklin, married Aug. 10, 1813, his father's and his mother's third cousin, Hannah Hyde, born Aug. 11, 1789, at Franklin, third daughter of Joseph Hyde and Susanna Waterman. They settled at Westerly, R. I., where she died. He had by her one child: Hezekiah, H., born 1814, died at the age of six years. He then went to Georgia and married in 1819, Sarah Gunby, of Columbus, Ga. He had by her two daughters: Mary and Sarah Elizabeth. One of them died in childhood, and the other married a commission merchant, at Savannah, by the name of Piper.

Carlos, born Aug. 8, 1793, at Franklin, married in 1822, Mrs. Jane D. (McLean) Givens, of Beaufort, S, C., born June, 1792, at Sanbury, Ga., daughter of Major Andrew McLean, of Savannah, Ga., and widow of —— Givens, of Beaufort. They settled at Beaufort, resided some time at Augusta, Ga., where he was a director of the bank. He was subsequently a commission merchant and factor at Charleston, S. C., and died in August, 1827, at Beaufort, and she died March 7, 1847. They had three children, all born at Beaufort: Jane, born March 8, 1824, was living in 1859, at Geneva, N. Y., unmarried; Carlos, born Sept. 1, 1825. He was a lawyer and settled at Walterboro, Colleton, district, S. C., where he was a member of the state legislature, and where he was living in 1860, unmarried: Clem Chandos, born Feb. 10, 1828. He was a lawyer, and pursued that profession for some years in the Beaufort district. He married Oct. 23, 1852, Emma H. Parker, a grand-daughter of Thomas Hayward, one of the signers of the Declaration of Independence. He afterwards relinquished the practice of law, and became the owner of the Poco Sabo plantation, near Ashapoe ferry, in the parish of St. Bartholomews, Colleton district, S. C., where he died June 17, 1859. They had three children: Eliza Parker, born Sept. 17, 1854; Carlos Chandos, born Jan, 27, 1856, and Jane, born in 1858.

Fitch Rogers, born March 30, 1806, at Franklin, married April 7, 1830. Charlotte Waldo Gager, born Sept. 28, 1807, at Franklin, daughter of Jason Gager and Esther his wife, of Franklin. They removed to Lapier county, Michigan, and in 1858, were living at Flint, in that county. They had ten children: Mortimer, born 1832, died in 1855, in California, unmarried; Joseph Chester, born in 1834, died in 1855, unmarried; Jane Elizabeth married Augustus Gregory, of Goodrichville; Emely married John Algoe; Caroline married Hiram Wilson; George Henry; William; Frederick; Melvin; Clarence Sophia.

Prudee, born Feb. 20, 1780, at Franklin, married Sept. 10, 1811, Joseph Chester, born Jan. 21, 1788, at Montville, second son of Joseph Chester and Elizabeth Lee, and fourth cousin by the Lee blood of her father and of her mother. [This Joseph Chester, (the father) born Jan. 27, 1758, at Montville, was the eldest son of Joseph Chester, Esq., of Montville, by his second wife, Elizabeth Otis, and had sixteen brothers and sisters, including one half-sister, Mary, whose mother was Rachael Hillhouse. He married Sept. 22, 1785, Elizabeth Lee, born May 25, 1757, at Lyme, and was killed at Montville, April 2, 1791, by the falling in of a rock, under the side of which he was excavating. His wife survived him, and died Jan. 6, 1843. She was the youngest daughter of Benjamin Lee, of Lyme, who was born Sept. 4, 1712, and married Jan. 25, 1735, Mary Ely, born Jan. 8, 1716, at Lyme, eldest daughter of Daniel Ely and Ann Champlin, and granddaughter of William Ely, the first, of Lyme, who was born in England. Benjamin Lee was the third son of John Lee and Elizabeth Smith, of Lyme, and grand-son of Lieut. Thomas Lee, the first, of Lyme, and his first wife, Sarah Kirkland.] Joseph Chester and Prudee Tracy, his wife, settled in 1812, at Chelsea Landing, now the city of Norwich, where he died Jan. 30, 1832. She had by him nine children, born at Norwich: Albert Tracy, born June 16, 1812. He graduated at Union College in 1834, was a Presbyterian clergyman and received the honorary degree of D. D. at Union in 1847. He married Aug. 3, 1836, Elizabeth Stanley, born Aug. 5, 1814, at Goshen, Conn., daughter of Oliver Stanley and Rhoda Powell, of Mount Morris, N. Y., a descendent of the seventh generation, of John Stanley, of Farmington, Conn., who was born January, 1624, in England, and came to America in 1634, with his father, John Stanley, and married Sarah Scott, daughter of Thomas Scott, one of the first settlers of Hartford. The Rev. Albert Tracy Chester was settled as pastor of the church at Ballston Spa, and afterwards as pastor of the church at Saratoga Springs, and in 1850 was settled as pastor of a church at Buffalo, N. Y., where they were living in 1859. They had nine children: Alice, born May 20, 1837, at Ballston Spa, married June 3, 1858, Hubert R. Ives, son of William Ives, of New Haven. They were living at Montreal in 1863, and had three children: Lillian, Nettie, and a son; Frank Stanley, born May 5, 1839, at Ballston Spa, captain of volunteers in 1861, married Dec. 24, 1861, Kate Stillman, of Buffalo. They were living at Buffalo in 1863, and had one daughter, Mabel: Walter Tracy, born July 31, 1841, at Saratoga Springs, lieutenant of volunteers in 1863; Albert Huntington, born Nov. 22, 1843, at Saratoga Springs, under graduate at Union in 1863; Elephelet Nott, born July 18, 1846, at Saratoga Springs; Elizabeth, born Nov. 7, 1848 at Saratoga Springs; Catherine, born Sept. 6. 1850, at Buffalo; Ellen, born Aug. 1852, at Buffalo; Walworth, born April 6, 1858, at Buffalo.

Harriet Newel, born Sept. 27, 1814, at Norwich, died April 23, 1715.

Charles Huntington, born Oct. 14, 1816, married June 8, 1841, his mother's third cousin, Julia Anna Thomas, born April 17, 1817, at Norwich, Conn., second daughter of Charles Thomas and Frances Nevens. He was a Presbyterian clergyman, and was settled at Greenfield, Schuylerville and Niagara Falls, N. Y. They were living at Geneva, N. Y., in 1857, and had eight children: William Nevens, born June 7, 1842, at Greenfield; Mary, born Sept. 24, 1843, at Greenfield, died March 28, 1844; Thomas born May 29, 1845, at Schuylerville; Sarah Elizabeth, born Jan. 15, 1847, at Schuylerville; Eliza, born Dec. 11, 1848, at Schuylerville; Carlos Tracy, born March 17, 1851, at Niagara Falls; Frederick, born May 19, 1853, at Niagara Falls; Clara, born May 14, 1855, at Niagara Falls.

Harriet Lee, born Jan. 31, 1819, at Norwich, died April 1, 1820.

Joseph Lemuel, born April 30, 1821, married June 26, 1839, Catherine Hendrickson Hubbard, born June 26, 1819, at New York, eldest daughter of John Hubbard and Eleanor Gustin Shepard. They were living at Philadelphia, Pa., in 1856, and had four children: Mary, born March 21, 1840, at Cleveland; Albert Horsford, born Oct. 14, 1841, at New York; Anna, born July 12, 1843, at New York; and Emma, born July 12, 1845, at Brooklyn.

Sarah Elizabeth, born Nov. 21, 1823, married June 16, 1846, Benjamin S. Stone, born March 26, 1821, at Bridgport, Vt., son of Isaac Stone and Lydia B. Hulbert, of Bridport. They settled at Mexico, N. Y., where they were living in 1856. They had four children: Walter Chester, born Dec. 27, 1847; Anne, born May 5, 1851, died Sept. 26, 1852; Edward Tracy, born April 28, 1852; William Gleason, born March 21, 1855.

Leonard Hendee, born Oct. 1, 1825, married Nov. 5, 1849, Lucy Caroline Thurston, born March 8, 1826, at Preston, Conn., daughter of Benjamin Tayler Thurston and Mary, his wife, of Norwich. They were living at Norwich in 1856, and had one child, Carl Linley, born August, 1853.

Anson Gleason, born July 25, 1827, graduated at Union college in 1849, and was an editor and miscellaneous writer. He married Nov. 21, 1852, Mary Tillie Staines, of Buffalo, born June 24, 1832, at Troy, N. Y., daughter of John Staines and Elizabeth his wife. They settled at Buffalo, where they were living in 1857, and had two children: Winfred Tracy, born Oct. 10, 1853, and Anson Couldock, born July 28, 1855.

Frank, born Jan. 19, 1830, at Norwich, and died Jan. 27, 1831.

After the death of her first husband Mrs. Prudee (Tracy) Chester removed in 1835, with most of her children, to Rome, O., where she married Sept, 6, 1837, Rev. John Hall, of Ashtabula, O., born Nov, 5, 1788. He was in early life engaged some years in teaching, in 1822 was ordained as a deacon, and in 1823, as a priest of the Episcopal church, and was settled as rector of St. Peter's church, at Ashtabula, O. She died Oct. 6, 1853, at Norwich, while on a visit to her friends there, and was burried by the side of her first husband. She had no issue by her second husband, who in 1853, was living at Ashtabula.

Cynthia, born March 13, 1790, at Franklin, married, March 15, 1809, her fifth cousin, Charles Huntington, born June 8, 1785, at Norwich, eldest son of Elisha Huntington and Nancy Rude, of Franklin. He died Oct. 19, 1816, at Norwich. She had by him four children: Joseph Pettis, born in 1810, who died in infancy; Cornelia Rude, born April 10, 1811, at Franklin, married Joseph H. Pettis. She was living at Brooklyn, N. Y., in 1858, and had three children; Carlos Tracy, born Aug. 6, 1813, at Franklin, married June 6, 1854, Ellen J. Cobb, of Norwich, and was a broker, living in New York in 1858; Nancy Rude, born Sept. 22, 1815, married George Howard, and was living at Tarrytown, N. Y., in 1858, and had three children. After the death of her first husband, Mrs. Cynthia Tracy Huntington married in 1829, Cornelius M. Paul, of Richfield, N. Y., and had by him two other children: Catherine M., born Feb. 18, 1830, died May 31, 1847, unmarried; and Cornelia. He died June 26, 1833, aged 36 years and 10 months, and his widow died about 1857, at Richfield.

Lydia, born May 15, 1795, at Franklin, married Jan. 1, 1815, Henry Fox, and died in 1830. They had five children: a son, who died in infancy; Prudce, who married Milton Delong, and removed to Clarion Valley, Pa.; Henry, who married and settled in Jefferson county, N. Y.; Elizabeth, and Caroline A., who was a teacher at the Lower Cattaraugus Indian Mission, N. Y. She married Hamlin B. Buckingham, of Norwich, librarian of the Otis Library, about 1858.

Rachel, born Jan. 4, 1797, at Franklin, married Jan, 8, 1815, Charles Pettis. They removed to Davidsonville, Mich., where he died March 4, 1845. She had by him eleven children: Eliza, who married, and was living at Flint, Mich., in 1858; Abby, who died in infancy; Rachel, who married Daniel O. Barney, and died, leaving one child, Rachel; Charles, who married Jane Annabel; Eleazer Tracy, who married Elsie Gorton; second Abby, who died unmarried; Julia, who married James Shields, and died leaving two children; Peter, who married Mosella D. Clark; Elizabeth Stanley, who married Henry Ball; Louisa, unmarried in 1858; Albert Chester, unmarried in 1858. After the death of her first husband, she married in 1852, Augustus Davidson, who died Nov. 22, 1854. She died in 1858, without issue by him.

Eliza, born May 11, 1798, at Franklin, married July 20, 1816, at Franklin, Joseph Crandall, of Sangersfield, N. Y., who died s. p. She then married in 1824, Israel Keith, of Georgia. She had by him two children: Anne Bennet, who married in 1840, her mother's third cousin, Robert T. Hyde, the youngest son of James Hyde and Elizabeth Starr, of Richfield, N. Y.; Nelson Baber, who was living at Geneva, N. Y., in 1858.

Elizabeth Hill, born June 11, 1800, at Franklin, died July, 1820, unmarried.

Margaret P., born Jan. 11, 1802, at Franklin, died in 1830, at Hamilton, N. Y., unmarried.

Bethia Williams, born June 20, 1803, at Franklin, married Oct. 24, 1826, Anson Gleason, born May 2, 1797, at Manchester, Conn. They went to Georgia, as Assistant Missionaries of the A. B. C. F. M., to the Choctaw Indians, and were released in

1831. He was afterwards ordained as a Congregational clergyman, and for some years preached to the Indians at Mohegan, Conn., and had charge of their school. In 1858 he was a missionary to the Seneca Indians at the Cattaragus Missionary Station, N. Y., and she was an assistant missionary and teacher. He was originally a mechanic, and had not the advantages of a liberal education. But he had very considerable power as a public speaker, was a warm and devoted friend to the Indians, and a most faithful minister of the gospel. They had eight children: Elizabeth Tracy, born Sept. 19, 1827, at Mayhew, married Nov. 17, 1849, Dana P. White, born November, 1826, and had in 1856, two children, Anna Lizzie and Mary Adda, born March 2, 1853; Mary Louisa, born July 24, 1829, at the Choctaw Mission, unmarried in 1856; Anna Burnham, born July 1, 1832, at Mohegan, unmarried in 1856; Alfred W., born Oct. 1, 1834, at Mohegan, living at Toledo, Ohio, in 1856, unmarried; Sarah Rebecca, born Sept. 20, 1836, at Mohegan, died Sept. 30, 1840; Andrew Williams, born Nov. 20, 1838, at Mohegan, unmarried in 1856; Adeline Maria, born Sept. 30, 1840, at Mohegan; Worthington Hooker, born March 8, 1844, at Mohegan, died Dec. 23, 1845.

Adaline, born July 26, 1807, at Franklin, married Nov. 26, 1829, Amen Wadsworth Langdon, born June 25. 1795, at Farmington, Conn., only child of Capt. Amon Langdon and Lucy Wadsworth, of Farmington. He was a merchant in Georgia for some years, and after his marriage they settled at Geneva, N. Y., where they were living in 1857. They had five children, all born at Geneva: Eliza Tracy, born Aug. 26, 1830, married Oct. 6, 1852, George W. Root, son of Timothy H. Root and Celestia Lewis, of Farmington, Conn. They were living at Phelps, N. Y., in 1757, and had one child, Amon Langdon, born May 1, 1855, at Phelps; George Curtis, born April 9, 1833. He was living at Detroit, in 1867, unmarried; Lucy Wadsworth, born March 30, 1835, married Sept. 3, 1856, Stephen H. Hammond, a lawyer, of Albany, N. Y., who, in 1857, was deputy attorney-general of the state of New York; Ella Chester, born May 5, 1838, was living with her parents in 1857, unmarried; Thomas Folger, born Dec. 24, 1843, at Geneva.

Julia Frances, born Aug. 10, 1709, at Franklin, married May 6, 1838, Rev. Daniel VanValkenberg, born Jan. 8, 1805, at Manheim, N. Y., son of James VanValkenberg and Elizabeth McConel. He graduated at Union College in 1824, was licensed as a Presbyterian clergyman in 1827, and ordained July 13, 1831. He was settled at Evans' Mills, Richfield Springs, Mexico, Taberg and Exeter, N. Y. They were living at Exeter, N. Y., in 1856. They had five children: Albert Chester, born May 2, 1839 died Aug. 29, 1839; Charles Huntington, born April 30, 1840, died April 28, 1847; Mary Warner, born Jan. 23, 1842; second Albert Chester, born Jan. 21, 1846; Helen Catherine, born Oct. 19, 1848.

Mary Hendee, born Nov. 3, 1811, at Franklin, married in July, 1840, James Henry Warner, of Williamsburgh, N. Y., where she died April 1, 1841, s. p.

Peter Tracy, born at Norwich, Conn., April 19, 1767, second son of Josiah Tracy, and Margaret Pettis, of Norwich, was a great grand-son of John Hyde, of the third generation. He married Nov. 30, 1788, his third cousin, Abigail Hartshorn, second daughter of Capt. Ebenezer Hartshorn and Abigail Barstow, of Franklin. He was a blacksmith, and they settled at Franklin, where he died July 3, 1830. She was living at Carlisle, N. Y., in 1857. Their children were; Dyer, born April 24, 1790, at Franklin, died May 27, 1790; second Dyer, born June 19, 1791, at Franklin, married in 1816, Desdamona Babcock, of Burlington, N. Y. She died. He was living at Albion, N. Y., in 1857. They had six children: three sons and three daughters, the particulars of whom I have not ascertained.

Simon, born May 3, 1795, at Franklin, married Nov. 21, 1818 Ruth Kingsbury, of Coventry, Conn., daughter of Joseph Kingsbury and Lois Porter, of Coventry. He was a merchant, and they settled at Lebanon and removed to Norwich, Conn., where she died Oct. 27, 1831. He had by her three children: Addison

Leander, born Oct. 25, 1819, at Lebanon, married Jan. 14, 1845, Laura P. Hunt, of Vernon, born about 1820, who died Aug. 3, 1846, at Rockville. He had by her one child, Theodore Hunt, born May 16, 1846. He then married April, 1848, Annie Lovice Chester, daughter of Socrates Chester, of Ellington. They were living at Elmwood, Ill., in 1857. He had by her two or three children: Mary Ruth, born January, 1849, died Nov. 19, 1851; Frederick, etc.

Lois Abby, born July 21, 1821, at Lebanon, married Aug. 24, 1842, Eli Griffith, born Dec. 2, 1818, at Ellington, son of Eli Griffith and Abby Booth. They were living at Ellington in 1857, and had five children: Alonzo Tracy, born Aug. 12, 1843; Ruth Louisa, born Jan. 10, 1846; George Fitch, born March 29, 1848; Ellen Maria, born Aug. 5, 1850; and Emma, born May 31, 1857.

Susan Kingsbury, born Oct. 23, 1831, at Norwich, was living at Elmwood, Ill., in 1857, unmarried. Simon Tracy then married March 15, 1833, Frances M. Adams, of Canterbury, where she died May 4, 1834, s. p. He then married Dec. 13, 1835, Elizabeth Abel, of Lisbon, daughter of Andrew Abel, of Hanover. They settled at Rockville, where he was engaged in manufacturing where he died May 11, 1854. She died Aug. 9, 1855. He had by her one child: Harlan Page, born March 2, 1840, at Rockville.

Ebenezer Hartshorn, born July 13, 1798, at Franklin. He went to western Virginia about 1817, and is supposed to have been killed by the Indians a few years afterwards in attempting to cross the Rocky mountains.

Peter, born July 16, 1800, at Franklin. He was brought up by his uncle, Abel Hyde, of Columbus, N. Y., and was for some years after he arrived at his majority, employed upon the public works. He married in 1832, Miranda Hall, born Jan. 16, 1816, at Hector, N. Y., daughter of Anson Hall and Lucy Taylor. They settled at Havana, N. Y., where he engaged in merchandise. They were living at Havana in 1857, and had eight children: Ellen, born Oct. 26, 1833, died April 25, 1836; Louisa C., born May 15, 1836, educated at the Troy Female Seminary, unmarried in 1857 ; Albert H., born April 29, 1839, died Feb. 16, 1857 ; George, born Feb. 18, 1843, died April 8, 1843 ; Charles A., born June 18, 1844 ; Calvin, born March, 1846, died in infancy ; Lucy Abby, born April 30, 1849 ; and Willie, born Jan. 15, 1852.

Andrew Williams, born April 7, 1805, at Franklin, married May 23, 1833, Emeline Talcott, daughter of Deacon Alvin Talcott and Philomela Root, of Vernon, Conn. He was a merchant and they were living at Rockville, Conn., in 1858. They had five children ; Emma L., born May 9, 1836, married July 2, 1856, Andrew Cotter Baldwin, born Oct. 6, 1831, son of Noah Baldwin and Sabia Smith Cotter, of Cornwall. They settled at West Cornwall, Conn., where he died Jan. 26, 1858 ; Rosa M., born Sept. 25, 1838. She was living with her parents in 1858, at Rockville, unmarried ; Mary Louisa, born Jan. 20, 1843, died Aug. 23, 1844 ; Alvan Talcott, born Jan. 2, 1845, at Rockville ; Louisa Adella, born Dec. 13, 1853, at Rockville.

Jabez Hartshorn, born July 18, 1810, at Franklin, married Dec. 30, 1832, Hannah Bailey Fillmore, born Feb. 20, 1814, at Franklin, daughter of his fourth cousin, Annice Bailey and the Rev. Comfort Day Fillmore, of Franklin. He was a manufacturer, and died Aug. 27, 1855, at Lisbon, Conn., where she was living in 1857. They had nine children ; Ellen Sophia, born Dec. 19, 1833 ; Edwin Day, born Feb. 19, 1836 ; Henry Fitch, born June 13, 1838 ; Emma Jane ; Jabez Addison ; William Huntington ; Mary Ann ; Ida Elizabeth ; Annice Louisa.

Sophia Williams, born Nov. 17, 1793, at Franklin, married her father's third cousin, Roswell Huntington, seventh son of Capt. Andrew Huntington and Ruth Hyde, of Lebanon.

Abby Barstow, born Aug. 26, 1802, at Franklin, married Nov. 1, 1821, Clark Davison, born at Hartwick, N. Y., son of Nathan Davison and Catherine, his wife. He was an extensive farmer, and they settled at Hartwick. They were living at Hartwick Seminary in 1857. They had seven children, all born at Hartwick: Anne Elizabeth, born Nov. 6, 1823, married Oct. 27, 1847, Rev. George H. Miller, son of Rev. George B. Miller and Delia B., his wife, of Hartwick Seminary. He died Jan. 19, 1850. She was living at Hartwick Seminary in 1857, and had one child, Francis Louisa, born Aug. 11, 1848; William Clark, born Jan. 1, 1826, living at Hartwick Seminary in 1857, unmarried; Albert Nathan, born June 10, 1828. He was living in California in 1857, unmarried: Catherine Louisa, born April 21, 1831, unmarried in 1857; Delia Tracy, born Dec. 11, 1833, died Dec. 25, 1834; Emma Sophia, born July 27, 1835, living at Hartwick Seminary in 1857, unmarried; second Delia Tracy, born April 1, 1838, unmarried in 1857.

Louisa, born Oct. 2, 18)8, at Franklin, married Calvin Cooley, a lumber merchant. They were living at Albany in 1859, sine prole.

Emma Elvira, born Jan. 6, 1813, at Franklin, married her fourth cousin, Alexander Fitch, second son of Dr. Benjamin Bissell Fitch and Esther Hyde, of Lebanon. They were living at New York in 1857, s. p.

Josiah Tracy, born at Norwich, Conn., May 7, 1772, third son of Josiah Tracy and Margaret Pettis, was a great grand-son of John Hyde, of the third generation. He married Feb. 20, 1796, Mary Birchard, born July 25, 1773, at Norwich, daughter of Jesse Birchard and Lydia Waterman, of Bozrah. He was a mechanic, and they settled at Franklin. They removed to Collumbus, N. Y., where she died Sept. 10, 1840, and he died April 3, 1844, at Honesdale, Pa. Their children were: Josiah, born Oct. 1, 1796, at Franklin, married Aug. 18, 1824, Diantha Lathrop, born about 1802, daughter of Eleazer Lathrop, from Connecticut, who was one of the earliest settlers of Sherburne, N. Y. They settled at Painsville, O., where he was engaged in mercantile business with one of his brothers and was a colonel of militia. In 1832 they removed to Vermillion, O., where he supertended the Huron company iron works, and was the first agent of that company. About 1835, they removed to Huron, and he was engaged in forwarding and commission business. He was mayor of Huron, a justice of the peace, a state senator, and one of the judges of Erie county. She died April 22, 1840, at Huron and he subsequently removed to Mansfield, O., where he died Jan. 11, 1857. They had seven children: Lathrop J., born May 26, 1825, at Painesville, married in 1852, Eliza Kirkland of Honesdale, Pa., and was living at Mansfield in 1857, and had two children: Eunice M., born April 4, 1829, died in 1830; Frederick E., born May 6, 1831, at Painesville, married in 1855, Anne Lord, of Honesdale, and was living at Zanesville in 1857, and had one child, Ruth M., born April 6, 1833, at Huron, died in 1734; Sarah F., born June 13, 1835, at Huron, died in 1839; Mary D., born Jan. 12, 1839, at Huron, unmarried in 1857, Frances, born April 10, 1840, died in infancy.

Jabez Avery, born April 26, 1798, at Franklin, married and settled at Painesville, O., where he was a merchant. He had two children: James and Catherine. He died Nov. 9, 1830, at Mansfield, O.

Guilford, born May 2, 1800, at Franklin, married April 1, 1823, Jane Mead, of New York. They removed to Honesdale, Pa,, where he died May 23, 1837, and she died June 2, 1828. They had two children: Helen Marr, born Jan. 6, 1827, at New York, married H. A. Clark, of Gilbertville, N. Y., and was living in Milwaukee in 1856; Mary Jane, born Feb. 9, 1834, at Honesdale, married September, 1855, Charles E. Havens, of Utica, N. Y., and was living in Milwaukee in 1856.

Thomas Howard Ray, born May 16, 1806, at Franhlin, married Aug. 19, 1832, Anna A. Aldrich, born July 25, 1809, at Sherburne, N. Y., daughter of James Aldrich and Sybil Curtis, of Sherburne. They settled at Honesdale, Pa. He had only a common school education, having spent his youth in laboring in his father's shop and on his farm. Soon after they settled at Honesdale, he was appointed superintendent of the Pennsylvania section of the Delaware and Hudson canal, which position he occupied until his death. He was one of the associate judges of Wayne county, and was for many years chief burgess of Honesdale. He was an humble and devoted christian, was kind and benevolent to the poor and suffering, and was prompt and liberal in the promotion of all public enterprises. He died May 5, 1856, at Honesdale, leaving her surviving. They had six children, all born at Honesdale: Anne Maria, born June 19, 1833, died Sept. 1, 1834; Miles Lathrop, born March 10, 1836; Catherine Seymour, born May 16, 1839; Charles Wurts, born July 19, 1843; Thomas Howard Ray, born Aug. 22, 1845; Lucy Ann, born Dec. 25, 1847.

Horace Hyde, born May 26, 1811, at Columbus, married May 28, 1846, Clarissa Tucker, daughter of Stephen Tucker and Lucy Harris, of Jackson, Pa. They settled at Honesdale, where he died June 9, 1844. She was living at Honesdale in 1856. They had two children, born at Honesdale: James Horace, born Feb. 22, 1845: and Clarissa Amelia, born Oct. 5, 1846, died April 3, 1851.

Ruth Maria, born March 21, 1802, at Franklin, married March, 1850, E. P. Sturgess, of Mansfield, O., where they were living in 1856, s. P.

Lucy Tracy, born at Norwich, Conn., Oct, 7, 1760, second daughter of Josiah Tracy and Margaret Pettis, of Norwich, was a great grand-daughter of John Hyde, of the third generation. She married Oct. 30, 1783, her father's second cousin, of the Tracy blood, Daniel Tracy, born Oct. 23, 1756, at Norwich, fourth son of Josiah Tracy, by his first wife, Rachel Allyn. [That Josiah Tracy was born May 10, 1718, at Norwich, and married Nov. 3, 1740, Rachel Allyn, born June 10, 1719, daughter of Timothy Allyn and Rachel Dushnell, of Norwich. He was the third son of Winslow Tracy and Rachel Ripley, of Norwich, which Winslow Tracy, born Feb. 8, 1689, was the youngest son of John Tracy, the first, of Norwich, and Mary Winslow.] They settled at Norwich, removed to Boston, and from there to Dover, N. H. She died Oct. 11, 1807. Their children were: Lucy, born Sept. 13, 1784, at Norwich, married Dr. Wheeler Palmer, a physician, and settled at Otsego, N. Y., and probably died s. p. He died Jan. 5, 1860, at Richfield Springs, N. Y. He had two other wives, Nancy, born Aug. 18, 1786, at Norwich, married March 8, 1808, at Franklin, Atkins Clark, of Boston, and they settled at Boston where he was a trunk-maker; Frances; Augusta, who died unmarried; Lucretia.

Lucretia Tracy, born at Norwich, Conn., Sept. 4, 1774, fifth daughter of Josiah Tracy and Margaret Pettis, was a great granddaughter of John Hyde, of the third generation. She married March 6, 1799, William Bailey, born June 6, 1768, son of Isaac Bailey and Alathea Torry, of Lebanon. They settled at Lebanon, where he died June 17, 1848. She was living at Rockville, Conn., in 1857. Their children were: Alonzo, born Dec. 14, 1799, at Lebanon, married Sept. 22, 1836, Lucinda Pease, born in 1816, daughter of Deacon Jonathan Pease and Eleanor Gleason, of Enfield. He obtained a divorce from her in 1855. He had by her three children: Lucinda, born Dec. 9, 1840; Eleanor Gleason, born June 13, 1844; Lucretia Tracy, born Oct. 28, 1846. He then married Jan. 15, 1857, Catherine Noble, daughter of Solomon Noble and Dorcas Vinton, of Mansfield. They were living at Rockville, Conn., in 1857, where he was the agent of a large manufacturing establishment.

William T., born April 25, 1804, at Lebanon, married Feb. 19, 1834, Mary Esther Clark, born in 1814, daughter of ———— Clark and Mehetable Hubbard, of Chatham. They settled at Buffalo, N. Y., where they were living in 1857. They had six children, all born at Buffalo: Earl William, born March 16, 1835; Mary Esther, born July 21, 1837; Alonzo Tracy, born Feb. 11, 1839; Chauncey Clark, born Nov. 21, 1840; Emely Hubbard, born July 7, 1842; William Watson, born April 16, 1846.

Dyer Y., born Feb. 4, 1808, at Lebanon, died Aug. 28, 1827, at Manhattan, O., unmarried.

Almanthe, born Dec. 10, 1801, at Lebanon, married Dec. 30, 1821, Delamere Smith, born Jan. 15, 1796, son of Shubal Smith, of Windham. He died Dec. 5, 1830. She had by him two children; Mary Ann, born Dec. 28, 1822, living at Chicago in 1857, unmarried; Eliza, born Dec. 16, 1825, married —— Hull, and living at Chicago in 1857. She then married Joseph K. Edgerton, born in 1815, who died June 18, 1836, s. p. She then married June 16, 1837, William P. Comstock, born June 16, 1809, at Lyme, Conn. She died May 11, 1847, and he was living at Chicago in 1857. She had by him four children: Saphronia Antoinette, born Dec. 10, 1838; Leonora Josephine, born about 1840; Emely D., born about 1843, died June 13, 1846; Mary Edna.

Lucretia, born Sept. 1, 1806, at Lebanon, married Sept. 1, 1840, Robert Champlain, born Jan. 23, 1805, son of John Champlain, of Lebanon. They were living at Lebanon in 1857, and had two children: Martha, born in October, 1841, and Henry.

Emely Wight, born Dec. 30, 1817, at Lebanon, married Sept. 1, 1840, Rufus Ripley Dimock, born July 25, 1814, son of Rufus Dimock and Elizabeth Ripley, of Mansfield. They were living at Rockville in 1857, s. p.

Rachel Tracy, born at Norwich, Conn., March 6, 1777, sixth daughter of Josiah Tracy and Margaret Pettis, was a great granddaughter of John Hyde, of the third generation. She married Jan. 19, 1797, Cyrenus Clark, born April 18, 1772, at Lebanon, son of Jarred Clark and her fourth cousin, Mary Abel. They removed to Cooperstown, N. Y., where they resided many years. In 1858 they were living with their son, James Henry Clark, at Winfield, N. Y. Their children were: Ezekiel Hyde, born July 9, 1801, at Cooperstown, married in 1827, Nancy Williams, of Otsego county. He was a tanner and currier, and was living at Maine, N. Y., in 1858.

Abel Hyde, born Jan. 14, 1804, at Cooperstown, married in 1830, Mary Elizabeth Earnst, of Cooperstown, who died in 1836. He was a merchant, and was living at La Crosse, Wisconsin, in 1858.

Josiah Tracy, born June 1, 1806, at Cooperstown, married in 1835, Sophia Perkins, of Michigan. He was a physician, and settled in Michigan, and died in 1849.

Harvey Fitch, born July 14, 1808, at Cooperstown, married in 1833, Lucy Pratt, of Cooperstown. He was a carpenter and builder, and was living at Dunkirk, N. Y., in 1858.

William, born June 25, 1811, at Cooperstown, married in 1836, Anne Maria Newkirk, of Palatine, N. Y., who died in 1854. He was a forwarding merchant, and was living at Fort Plain in 1858, and had been a member of the legislature.

James E., born July 6, 1813, at Cooperstown, and died in 1816.

James Henry, born June 10, 1815, at Cooperstown, married Sept. 17, 1840, Angaline Cook, daughter of Otis Cook and Lydia Cass, of Exeter, N. Y He was a farmer, and they settled at Winfield, N. Y., where she died Oct. 17, 1847. He had by her two children, born at Winfield: Otis Henry Cyrenus, born Nov. 4, 1843; Almond Crandall, born April 29, 1847. He then married June 10, 1852, at Bradford, Wis., Jane Wetmore, born Sept. 7, 1828, at Winfield, daughter of Richard Wetmore and Electa Reed. They were living at Winfield in 1858. He had by her three children, born at Winfield: Frederick James, born April 19, 1853; Richard Tracy, born Dec. 11, 1854; George Irving, born Nov. 18, 1856.

John Augustus, born Aug, 9, 1817, at Cooperstown, married Sept. 9, 1846, Laura Cornelia Pomeroy, daughter of Dr. George Pomeroy and Ann Cooper, of Cooperstown, and niece of Fenimore Cooper, the novelist. He was a farmer, and in 1858, was living at Green Lake, Wis.

Emma Elvira, born Aug. 20, 1798, at Cooperstown, and died abovt 1812.

Naoma Tracy, born at Norwich, Conn., May 17, 1708, seventh daughter of Josiah Tracy, and Margaret Pettis, was a great grand-daughter of John Hyde, of the third generation. She married Sept. 14, 1802, Deacon Joseph H. Willes, born June 15, 1781, youngest son of Joshua Willes, of Norwich, by his second wife, Eunice Huntington, of Lebanon. [This Joshua Willes, born Aug. 28, 1735, at Norwich, who married Sept. 30, 1760,

'Martha Edgerton; married Dec. 13, 1764, Eunice Huntington, and had by her two sons and two daughters: Jabez, Joseph H., Temperance and Martha; married Feb. 14, 1793, Elizabeth Bushnell, of Lisbon, and died Dec. 2, 1815, aged 80 years, was the youngest son of the Rev. Henry Willes and Martha Kirtland, of Norwich. The Rev. Henry Willes, son of Jashua Willes, of Windham, died in January, 1721, at the age of 75 years. He graduated at Yale in 1715, and in October, 1718, was ordained, and settled as the first minister of the church at Norwich, West Farms, now Franklin. He married Oct. 27, 1718, Martha Kirtland, and died Sept. 30, 1758, at Norwich, and she died Dec. 11, 1773. They had nine children: John, born in 1719, died the same month; Martha, born April 20, 1721, married in 1753, Jabez Edgerton; Parnal, born March 14, 1723, married Simon Abel; Lydia, born Nov. 25, 1125, died Dec 16, 1816, unmarried; Henry, born Jan. 20, 1728, died Jan. 21, 1796, unmarried; Hannah, born July 13, 1730, married Simon Peck: Ruth, born Jan. 21, 1733: Joshua, above named who married three wives; Temperance, born May 19, 1738, married Abner Hyde.] Deacon Joseph H. Willes and wife, settled at Franklin, where she died July 3, 1859, leaving him surviving. Their children were: Joseph Hunt Chappel, born April 5, 1804, at Franklin, died July 7, 1820, unmarried.

Josiah Tracy, born Jan. 20, 1810, at Franklin, died Nov. 30, 1843, unmarried.

Herman Huntington, born July 22, 1812, at Franklin, married April 5, 1835, his first cousin, the widow Mary Abel (Willes] Woodward, born Nov. 5, 1807, at Franklin, second daughter of Jabez Willes and Abigail Abel. They settled at Franklin, where they were living in 1859. He had by her five children, born at Franklin: Joseph J., born Feb. 26. 1836, died Feb. 28, 1842; Herman Tracy, born Oct. 9, 1840, died Dec. 28, 1842; Mary Naomi, born April 26, 1843: Harriet Tracy, born Dec. 25, 1845, died Jan. 16, 1849: James Warner, born June 10, 1848, died Feb. 6, 1849, at Franklin.

Joshua Henry, born March 25, 1824, at Franklin, died April 26, 1830.

Anson Gleason, born Oct. 7, 1826, at Franklin, died April 4, 1827.

Lucy Peck, born April 20, 1806, at Franklin, died May 14, 1821, unmarried.

Floretta Perkins, born April 22, 1808, married Sept. 14, 1828, her first cousin, Horatio Willes, born April 26, 1800, at Franklin, youngest son of Jabez Willes and Abigail Abel, of Franklin. She died Sept. 14, 1839, at Norwich. She had one child, Celia Susan, born June 7, 1829.

Hermoine Warner, born July 22, 1812, (twin to Herman H,) died April 1, 1813.

Catherine Jane, born April 17, 1817, at Franklin, died April 9, 1835, unmarried.

Margaret Selina Elmict, born March 14, 1821, at Franklin, married Nov. 13, 1839, George Avery of Norwich, and removed to one of the western states. They had one child recorded at Franklin, Margaret Olivia, born Oct. 2, 1840.

Dudley Tracy, born at Norwich, Conn., Sept. 28, 1760, eldest son of Lieut. Hezekiah Tracy, of Norwich, by his first wife, Elizabeth Pettis, was a great grand-son of John Hyde, of the third generation. He married Nov 3, 1783, Mary Kingsbury, of Norwich, daughter of Asa Kingsbury. They settled at Franklin, where he was a member of the state legislature. Their children were: Dudley, born Jan. 8, 1786, at Franklin, married April 17, 1811, Emma Ellis, of Franklin. They had two children recorded at Franklin: Joseph Peck, born April 9, 1812, at Franklin; Asa, born March 31, 1816, at Franklin: Chandler, born June 9, 1788, at Franklin; Uriah, born Nov. 1, 1792, at Franklin; Asahel, born July 7, 1795, at Franklin; Horatio, born March 27, 18.3), at Franklin, unmarried in 1857; Asa Kingsbury, born Feb. 6, 1804, at Franklin, died in 1819; Elizabeth, born Aug. 29, 1790, at Franklin, died in 1839, unmarried; Sarah, born Aug. 6, 1797, at Franklin, died in 1820, unmarried; Lucy C., born Dec. 22

1802, at Franklin, died in 1858, unmarried; Caroline A., born Jan. 24, 1808, at Franklin, unmarried in 1857.

Joshua Tracy, born at Norwich, Conn., Oct. 16, 1768, second son of Lieut. Hezekiah Tracy, of Norwich, by his first wife, Elizabeth Pettis, was a great grand-son of John Hyde, of the third generation. He married June 21, 1789, Sarah Payne, of Lebanon, born about 1772. They settled at Franklin, Conn., where he was twice elected to the legislature. She died June 25, 1821, at Franklin, aged 49 years. He then married Dec. 26, 1824, the widow Martha (Smith) Hastings, and died Aug. 9, 1834, at Franklin, without issue by her. She died Jan. 2, 1842. His children by his first wife were: Stephen, born Sept. 13, 1790, at Franklin married Oct. 9, 1814, his fourth cousin, Sarah Hyde, born Aug. 2, 1775, at Franklin, eldest daughter of Abel Hyde and Chloe, his wife. He was a blacksmith, and they settled at Franklin, where she died. He had by her five children, born at Franklin: Martha Marvin, born Jan. 31, 1815, married Sept. 4, 1836, David H. Waterman, of Bozrah; Saphronia Fuller, born Jan. 9, 1816, died unmarried; Chester Payne, born Aug. 14, 1817, died Feb. 5, 1818; Marvin, died in childhood. He then married Sarah Anne (Scovel) Foote, widow of Daniel Foote, and daughter of Solomon Scovel, Esq., of Colchester. He had by her three children: Harriet, Eunice and Elizabeth.

Hezekiah, born Feb. 27, 1792, at Franklin, married Caroline Hall, of Lebanon, Conn., and removed to Salina, N. Y., and had several children, whose names I have not obtained.

Marvin, born Aug. 21, 1798, at Franklin, married, and removed to Ohio.

Horatio Nelson, born May 26, 1800, at Franklin, married Sept. 16, 1822, Hetty Ann Birchard. He was a lieutenant in the United States revenue service, and his family were living at Norwich in 1857. He had two daughters: Sarah Ann, born July 25, 1823; Lucretia.

Henry Brown, born Sept. 22, 1805, at Franklin, married April 5, 1838, Caroline Backus.

Joshua, born Oct. 15, 1808, at Franklin, married March 20, 1833, Abby J. Hoxie, of Lebanon. They settled at Franklin and he represented that town in the state legislature one year. They had two children recorded at Franklin: Henry Nelson, born Jan. 4, 1834; Jane Ellen, born March 11, 1843.

Martha, born May 21, 1795, at Franklin, died in 1797.

Wealthea, born Aug. 26, 1802, at Franklin, married Feb. 27, 1823, Abial B. Sherman, of Nerwich, where he was living in 1860.

Eunice Eliza, born Aug. 13, 1811, at Franklin, married her fourth cousin, James Hazen Hyde, eldest son of Amasa Hyde and Anna Hazen, of Franklin.

Uri Tracy, born at Norwich, Conn., Feb. 8, 1764, eldest son of Daniel Tracy and Mary Johnson, of Norwich, was a great grand-son of John Hyde, of the third generation. He graduated at Yale in 1789. He engaged in teaching and became the principal of the Academy, at Oxford, N. Y. He married Ruth Hovey, of Oxford, where he settled and was a member of Congress. He died in 1838. Their children were: Samuel Miles, born at Oxford, graduated at Hamilton College in 1815, was a lawyer, and married Oct. 13, 1822, Mary Daley. They settled at Portsmouth, O., where she died Nov. 5, 1845, and he died Dec. 25, 1856. They had five children: Elizabeth Daley, born Aug. 4, 1823, married Jan. 29, 1843, Matthias B. Ross; Mary Ruth, born Dec. 16, 1825, married George Johnson, of Steubenville, O.; Samuel Uri, born Dec. 13, 1827, died May 1, 1835; William Daley, born July 30, 1833, died unmarried; Emely Anne, born Nov. 30, 1836.

Otis J., born at Oxford, married Margaret Cushman, who died. He then married Jan. 2, 1820, his father's third cousin, Jane Hyde, born March 9, 1802, at Franklin, youngest daughter of Joseph Hyde and Susanna Waterman. She died. He had by her one child, Joseph Otis. He then married Margaret Storms and died in August, 1849, at Oxford.

Uri, born Jan. 22, 1810, at Oxford, married Persis Packer, daughter of William Packer, of Preston, N. Y., and died April,

1856, at Oxford. They had four children: Susan Hosmer, married John H. Morris, of Syracuse; Charles Packer, born Dec. 5, 1829; Henry Reed; John Bailey.

Charles Oscar, born October, 1805, at Oxford, married in 1827, Maria Kinney. He was a lawyer, and they settled at Portsmouth, O. They had nine children: Francis Henry, born April 18, 1828, married Frances Oakes, of Portsmouth; Vander Lyn, born Oct. 11, 1829, married Annice Davis; Uri, born June 16, 1831; Mary Kinney, born March 23, 1833, married George Sutherland, of Danville, Va.; Anne Elizabeth, born May 13, 1835, died Oct. 4, 1836; Anne Maria, born Feb. 6, 1837, married John Davis, of Portsmouth; Persis, born June 26, 1839, died young; Charles Oscar, born April 15, 1843, died Sept. 17, 1844; Alice Ruth, born Jan. 29, 1845.

Mary, born at Oxford, married Peter Dickinson, of Baltimore, Md.

Hiel Tracy, born at Norwich, Conn., July 5, 1766, second son of Daniel Tracy and Mary Johnson, was a great grand-son of John Hyde, of the third generation. He married Nov. 8, 1795, his second cousin, Susanna Gifford, born March 10, 1771, at Norwich, second daughter of James Gifford and Susanna Hubbard. They settled at Franklin, and afterwards removed to Oxford, N. Y., in 1801, where he died Jan. 17, 1842, and where she died May 22, 1857. Their children were: Melissa, born Aug. 8, 1798, at Franklin, married Ebenezer Havens, and they were living at Dix, Schuyler county, N. Y., in 1861, and had four children: Anne E., Hiel Tracy, Albert and Ebenezer.

Eliza, born Oct. 26, 1800, at Franklin, married November, 1821, John Green, of Oxford, N. Y., born Nov. 10, 1776, and died Aug. 30, 1824. They had five children, born at Oxford: Susan Eliza, born Feb. 16, 1823, married Abner R. Holcomb, and had three children: Lucy Ann, born Dec. 6, 1825, married May 17, 1848, Wilson G. Mowry, of Woodhull, N. Y., and had three children; John M., born April 7, 1828, married Dec. 17, 1856, Mary E. Townsend, and were living at Oxford in 1860; Mary M., born

Oct. 27, 1830, died Jan 6, 1832; Martha V., born Dec. 23, 1832, died Oct. 10, 1833.

Susan, born July 30, 1802, at Oxford, married Ira Miner Maine, of Brookfield, N. Y. He was a farmer, and they were living at Orange, N. Y., in 1860, and had two children: Tracy M. and Uri H.

Sophia, born June 12, 1811, at Oxford, married in 1845, Dyer McCall. They were living at Oxford in 1860. He was a farmer, and they had one child: Olive E., born March 2, 1846.

James Tracy, born at Norwich, Conn., Feb. 9, 1770, third son of Daniel Tracy and Mary Johnson, was a great grand-son of John Hyde of the third generation. He married Ruth Calkins. His children by her were: Daniel, died in 1841, unmarried; Hiel; Eliza, born Oct. 9, 1792, died April 6, 1799; Sophia, married John Hillman, of Scipio, N. Y. He, James Tracy, then married Margaret Wheeler. His children by her were: James, died in 1818, unmarried; Elijah, married Caroline Havens, and settled at Dix, N. Y., and had four children: Jane, Ophelia, Phebe and Ellen; John Foote, married Ellen Jane Clark, and settled at New York, and had two children, Mary Jane and Ellen Jane; Lorenzo Lewis, married Phebe Jackson and settled at Dix, N. Y., and had three children: Benjamin, James and William; Charles, born in 1813, died in 1815; William died in 1820; Nathaniel; Sarah, married Orin Sharp, of Newfield, N. Y.; Lydia; Ethelinda; Margaret Jane.

Dtniel Tracy, born at Norwich, Conn., Aug. 3, 1774, youngest son of Daniel Tracy and Mary Johnson, was a great grandson of John Hyde, of the third generation. He married Mary Havens. Their children were: Johnson, married Lydia Beverly; Ira; Albert; Daniel; Ebenezer; Sylvanus; John; Eunice, married Cyrus Maine.

Theophilus Tracy, born at Norwich, Conn., Nov. 16, 1768, eldest son of Theopilus Tracy and Sarah Gifford, was a great grand-son of John Hyde, of the third generation. He married May 27, 1794, Thankful Draper. They removed to Pompey, N.

Y., in 1797. Their children were Samuel, born Nov. 3, 1798, at Pompey, married Feb. 7, 1829, Hannah Edwards. They had six children: Mary Jane, born March 2, 1830; William, born May 12, 1832; Sarah Anne, born March 27, 1834, died Sept. 20, 1834; Edward, born May 16, 1835; Hiel, born May 10, 1837; Charles Elijah, born March 5, 1841.

Theophilus Draper, born April 21, 1802, at Pompey, married Jan. 8, 1823, Patience Kenyon. They had six children: Marcia Adaline, born Dec. 1, 1827; Lucy Emeline, born July 27, 1830; Gifford Theophilus, born Oct. 4, 1833; Horace Fayette, born Aug. 11, 1836; John, born Oct. 25, 1839; Samantha, born Aug. 23, 1842.

Eri, born Dec 19, 1803, at Pompey, married Mary Hitchcock. They had five children: Saphronia Elizabeth, who died in childhood; Uri; Alpheus; Mary Malvina; second Saphronia Elizabeth.

Nehemiah, born March 15, 1808, at Pompey, died the same day.

William Henry, born April 16, 1809, at Pompey, died June 2, 1825, unmarried.

Riel Stephen, born June 27, 1811, at Pompey, married April 5, 1828, Adelia Robinson, who died Jan. 5, 1839, sine prole. He then married Dorothy Fairbanks, and had by her three children: Dorothy Adelia, born July 22, 1840; Stephen, born Oct, 18, 1841, died May 13, 1843; Frances Orcelia, born Oct. 28, 1843.

Experience, born March 3, 1795, at Pompey, died March 14, 1815, unmarried.

Anna, born Nov. 2, 1796, at Pompey, died Dec. 29, 1796.

Laura, born July 5, 1800, at Pompey, who married David Kenyon.

Thankful, born Dec. 19, 1803, at Pompey, (twin of Eri) married Orson Wheaton.

Joanna, born Nov. 13, 1813, at Pompey, married, Dec. 29, 1825, Murphy Thompson.

Riel Tracy, born at Norwich, Conn., Dec. 5, 1774, second son of Theophilus Tracy and Sarah Gifford, was a great grand-son of John Hyde, of the third generation. He married Dimis Anne Martin, and settled at Granville, N. Y. Their children were: Peter, William, Riel Huntington, Lucinda, Mary, Elmira and Dimis Anne.

Stephen Tracy, born at Norwich, Conn., Nov. 4, 1776, third son of Theophilus Tracy and Sarah Gifford, was a great grandson of John Hyde, of the third generation. He married the widow Wade, mother of the Rev. Jonathan Wade, the Baptist missionary. They settled at Hector, N. Y. Their children were: Allen, Theophilus, Horace.

Zebulon Edgerton, born at Norwich, Conn., March 4, 1755, eldest son of Zebulon Edgerton and Elizabeth Tracy, of Norwich, was a great grand-son of John Hyde of the third generation. He married about 1778, Abigail ———, and settled in that part of Norwich which was afterwards Franklin, and had five children recorded to them. Those children were: Reuben, Born May 29, 1779, at Norwich; Levi, born June 14, 1781, at Norwich; Whiting, born Feb. 28, 1785, at Norwich, Lydia, born July 9, 1783, at Norwich; Ruth, born March 26, 1793, at Franklin.

Bethia Edgerton, born at Norwich, Conn., Sept. 8, 1764, fifth daughter of Zebulon Edgerton and Elizabeth Tracy, was a great grand-daughter of John Hyde, of the third generation. She probably married Oct. 12, 1788, at Franklin, Elephelet Metcalf, born Jan. 28, 1763, at Lebanon, second son of her fourth cousin, Abel Metcalf, and Abigail Throop, of Lebanon. They settled at Franklin, where they had four children recorded to them. Those children were: Uri, born Dec. 31, 1788, at Franklin; Elephelet, born Nov. 19, 1792, at Franklin; Ira, born Sept. 10, 1794, at Franklin; Harriet, born Nov. 4, 1798, at Franklin, probably married Jan. 29, 1822, Samuel Huntington, of Lebanon.

Asa Waterman, born at Norwich, Conn., Dec. 2, 1772, eldest son of Arunah Waterman and Hannah Leffingwell, of Johnson, Vt., was a great grand-son of John Hyde, of the third generation. He married March 6, 1806, at Sterling, Vt., Anna McConnell, born April 23, 1784, at Piermont, N. H., daughter of Thomas McConnell. He was a farmer, and they settled at Johnson, Vt., where she died about 1813. His children by her were: Erastus, born Feb. 27, 1807, at Johnson, married, and was living in Michigan in 1856; Arunah, born Feb. 22, 1809, at Johnson. He went to Texas while a young man, where he probably died unmarried; Harvey, born Feb. 29, 1811, at Johnson. He was living at New York in 1856, unmarried; Thomas P., born April 20, 1813, at Johnson, died June 11, 1815. He then married Feb. 25, 1815, Anna Dodge, of Johnson, born March 3, 1784, at New Boston, N. H., daughter of Elisha Dodge and Ginger Raymond, formerly of Beverly, Mass. They were living at Johnson in 1857.

Caleb Abel, born at Norwich, Conn., April, 1677, second son of Caleb Abel and Margaret Post, of Norwich, was a grand-son of John Post, the first, and Hester Hyde, of Norwich. He married Feb. 20, 1705, Abigail Sluman, born March 14, 1689, at Norwich, daughter of Thomas Sluman and Sarah Bliss, of Norwich. They settled at Lebanon, where she died Nov. 11, 1748. The date of his death has not been ascertained. Their children were: Daniel, born Feb. 3, 1706, at Lebanon, married Sarah Crane; Caleb, born April 25, 1709, at Lebanon, married Mary Clark; Abigail, born April 11, 1711, at Lebanon, married Joseph Sluman; Mary, born Aug. 4, 1714, at Lebanon, living at Lebanon, where she died Feb. 26, 1785, unmarried.

John Abel, born at Norwich, Conn., December, 1678, third son of Caleb Abel and Margaret Post, of Norwich, was a grandson of John Post, the first, and Hester Hyde, of Norwich. He married June 2, 1703, Rebecca Sluman, born Oct. 3, 1682, at Norwich, daughter of Thomas Sluman and Mary Bliss, of Norwich. They settled at Lebanon. The dates and places of their deaths I have not ascertained. Their children were: John, born March 10, 1704, died same day; Solomon, born Jan. 7, 1708, at Lebanon, married Mary Northum; David, born April 7, 1722, at Lebanon, married Alice Roberts; Sarah, born March 2, 1705, at Lebanon, married Benjamin Metcalf; Rebecca, born Jan. 18, 1711, at Lebanon, married John West ; Bethia, born Oct. 18, 1713, at Lebanon ; Hannah, born Sept. 26, 1716, at Lebanon, married Oct. 3, 1739, Marshall Hackley, of Lebanon, and had a family. Their son Samuel, born Oct. 1, 1740, at Lebanon.

Theophilus Abel, born at Norwich, Conn., November, 1680, fourth son of Caleb Abel and Margaret Post, of Norwich, was a grand-son of John Post, the first, and Hester Hyde. He married June 27, 1716, Anne Calkins, born Oct. 10, 1692, at Norwich, eldest daughter of Hugh Calkins and Sarah Sluman, of Norwich, and grand-daughter of John Calkins and Sarah, his wife. Their children were : Anne, born July 2, 1717, at Norwich, married Hezekiah Edgerton ; Zerviah, born Jan. 29, 1722, at Norwich, married Elisha Edgerton.

Benjamin Abel, born at Norwich, Conn., ———, 1687, fifth son of Caleb Abel and Margaret Post, of Norwich, was a grandson of John Post, the first and Hester Hyde, of Norwich. He married March 17, 1714, Lydia Hazen. I suppose they settled in that part of Norwich which is now Franklin, but I have not ascertained the particulars of their residence and deaths. Their children were : Benjamin, born May 23, 1715, at Norwich, married Abigail Gild ; Andrew, born April 1, 1717, at Norwich, married his first cousin, Elizabeth Tracy ; Simon, born Sept. 15, 1721, at Norwich, married Parnal Willes ; Elijah, born May 12, 1729, at Norwich, married first, Anne Lathrop, second, Mary Cleveland ; Matthew, born Sept. 8, 1731, at Norwich ; Oliver, born Feb. 6, 1734, at Norwich, married Abigail Pettis ; Isaiah, born July 24, 1738, at Norwich, married Rhoda Pettis ; Lydia, born July 28, 1719, at Norwich, married her father's second cousin, Jabez Hyde, eldest son of Jabez Hyde and Elizabeth Bushnell ; Alice, born Jan. 14, 1724, at Norwich, had an illegitimate child in 1769, and probably died unmarried ; Hannah, born March 26, 1727, at Norwich, married Simeon Lathrop.

Mary Abel, born at Norwich, Conn., about 1685, the fourth daughter of Caleb Abel and Margaret Post, of Norwich, was a grand-daughter of John Post, the first, and Hester Hyde, of Norwich. She married Dec. 31, 1705, Capt. Joseph Tracy, born April 20, 1682, at Norwich, third son of John Tracy, the first, and Mary Winslow. They settled at Norwich, where he was a justice of the peace, and one of the leading men of the place. And he very frequently represented his native town in colonial legislature. His wife died Jan. 17, 1751. He survived her and died April 10, 1765, aged 83 years. Their children were: Joseph born Oct. 17, 1706, at Norwich, married Ann Hinckley; Elisha, born May 17, 1712, at Norwich, married first, Lucy Huntington, second, Elizabeth Dorr, third, widow Lois Huntington; Phinehas, born Jan. 1, 1721, at Norwich, died unmarried; Mary, born Jan. 4, 1708, at Norwich, married Benjamin Wadsworth, and is supposed to have died s. p.: Margaret, born May 11, 1710, at Norwich, married her second cousin, William Waterman; Zerviah; born Dec. 14, 1714, at Norwich, probably died unmarried; Lydia, born Dec. 10, 1716, at Norwich, married her mother's second cousin, Elisha Hyde; Irene, born Jan. 15, 1719, at Norwich, married Dec. 20, 1743, Daniel Burnham; Jerusha, born May 23, 1723, at Norwich, married her mother's second cousin, the Rev. Jedediah Hyde, fifth son of William Hyde; Elizabeth, born at Norwich, probably married her first cousin, Andrew Abel, born April 1, 1717, at Norwich, second son of Benjamin Abel and Lydia Hazen, of Norwich. He died Aug. 31, 1796, at Franklin. They had a son, Benjamin Abel, who married April 8, 1759, Esther Smith, and had five children, born at Norwich: Anne, born Oct. 7, 1760; Asa, born March 20, 1762; Solomon, born June 23, 1767; Elizabeth, born March 30, 1769; Rodolphus, born Nov. 26, 1770.

Abigail Abel, born at Norwich, Conn., March 16, 1690, fifth daughter of Caleb Abel and Margaret Post, was a grand-daughter of John Post and Hester Hyde. She married Jan. 12, 1710, Barnabas Lathrop. They settled at Norwich, where he died May 25, 1710. Her child by him was: Abigail, born Jan. 1, 1711, at Norwich. She then married Feb. 4, 1718, Christopher Huntington, born Sept. 12, 1686, at Norwich, by his wife, Sarah Adgate. [This Deacon Chistopher Huntington, was born Nov. 1, 1660, and was the first white male child born in Norwich. He was a son of Christopher Huntington and Ruth Rockwell, one of the 35 original proprietors of Norwich, who came from England to Roxbury in 1633, and married Oct. 7, 1652, Ruth Rockwell, eldest daughter of William Rockwell and Susanna Chapin, of Windsor. Sarah Adgate, the wife of Deacon Christopher Huntington, was born January, 1663, at Norwich, daughter of the first Deacon Thomas Adgate, one of the 35 proprietors of Norwich, by his second wife, the widow Sarah Bushnell.] Christopher Huntington and Abigail, his wife, settled at Norwich, where she died June 2, 1730. Her children by him were: Christopher, born June 20, 1719, at Norwich, married Sarah Bingham ; Elisha born Sept. 22, 1720, at Norwich, married Dinah Chapman ; Azariah, born Nov. 26, 1723, at Norwich, probably died unmarried ; Theophilus, born Sept. 12, 1726, at Norwich, married Lois Gifford, daughter of Samuel Gifford and Experience Hyde ; Barnabas, born May 29, 1728, at Norwich, married Anne Wright ; Ruth born Aug. 3, 1722, at Norwich, married Sept. 10, 1741, Joshua Sluman, who died Oct. 19, 1742, and she died Dec. 17, 1742, s. p. ; Margaret, born Nov. 23, 1724, at Norwich, married her third cousin, John Tracy, eldest son of John Tracy and Margaret Hyde ; Sarah, born April 27, 1731, at Norwich, married May 12, 1756, Asa Kingsbury, of Norwich, West Farms, now Franklin, born April 7, 1729, eldest son of Ephriam Kingsbury and Martha Smith. He died Sept. 5, 1775. They had four children recorded at Norwich ; Asa, born March 12, 1757 ; Sarah, born April 8, 1761 ; and Lucy, born June 20, 1771. After the death of his first wife, Christopher Huntington married May 2, 1783, Elizabeth Ensworth, of Canterbury, who died March 2, 1785, and had by her one daughter, Elizabeth, born Feb. 3, 1785, who died Oct. 25, 1758, unmarried. He then married June 4, 1740, Mary Brewster, who died Dec. 24, 1749. He then married Feb. 7, 1751, Mrs. Mary Gaylord, of Hebron, who died March 14, 1761, and he died Feb. 11, 1759.

Capt. John Hough, born at New London, Conn., Oct. 1, 1697, eldest son of Capt. John Hough and Sarah Post, of New London, was a grand-son of John Post, the first, and Hester Hyde, of Norwich. He married Sept. 4, 1718, Hannah Denison, born March 28, 1699, at New London, eldest daughter of George Denison, Esq., and Mary Witherell, of New London. [This George Denison, Esq., of New London, was a son of John Denison and Phebe Lay, of Stonington, and a grand-son of Capt. George Denison and Anne Borrodill, of Stonington. He graduated at Harvard in 1693, and was a lawyer, and for several years a clerk of the county court of New London county. He was born March 28, 1671, at Stonington, and died Jan. 20, 1720, at New London. He had eight children: Grace, born in 1695, married Edward Hallam; Phebe, born in 1697, married Gibson Harris; Hannah, born in 1699, married John Hough; Borrodill, born in 1701, married Jonathan Latimer; Daniel, born in 1703, married Rachel Starr; Wetherell, born in 1705, married Lydia Moore; Anne, born in 1707, married Samuel Richards; Sarah, born in 1709, married William Douglass.] They settled at New London, and removed to that part of Norwich, which is now Bozrah, where she died April 9, 1782.

Elijah Abel, born at Norwich, Conn., May 12, 1729, fourth son of Benjamin Abel and Lydia Hazen, of Norwich, was a great grand-son of John Post and Esther Hyde, of Norwich. He married Nov. 11, 1754, Ann Lathrop, born Feb. 15, 1731, third daughter of Capt. Ebenezer Lathrop and Lydia Leffingwell, and granddaughter of Thomas Leffingwell, the third, and Lydia Tracy, of Norwich. They settled at Norwich, where she died Dec. 15, 1764. His children by her were: Elijah, born Oct. 18, 1755, at Norwich; Abel, born Sept. 14, 1757, at Norwich; Jabez, born Oct. 17, 1759, at Norwich, probably married Jan. 18, 1795, Elizabeth Sanford; Anne, born April 3, 1762, at Norwich; Eunice, born March 7, 1764, at Norwich, probably married April 7, 1793, Oliver Smith, of Franklin. He then married Oct. 30, 1768, Mary Cleveland, and probably died at Norwich. But I have no further particulars as to his residence or the time and place of his death. His children by her were: Benjamin, born May 13, 1771, at Norwich; Elizabeth, born March 19, 1769, at Norwich, married Ozias Backus.

Oliver Abel, born at Norwich, Conn., Feb. 6, 1734, sixth son of Benjamin Abel and Lydia Hazen, of Norwich, was a great grand-son of John Post and Hester Hyde, of Norwich. He married Feb. 26, 1769, Abigail Pettis, born about 1746. They settled at Norwich, West Farms, now Franklin, where he died Nov. 12, 1815, and she died Dec, 14, 1823. Their children were: Oliver, born April 16, 1773, at Norwich, probably married Nov. 19, 1799, Mary Lord, of Franklin; Hiel, born Oct. 20, 1776, at Norwich, married Nov. 26, 1801, Cynthia Peck, and removed to Topsham, Me·; Asa, born Sept. 19, 1780, at Norwich, probably married first, Aug. 16, 1804, Clarissa Hewitt, of Franklin, second March 28, 1811, Charlotte Kingsbury, of Norwich: Benjamin, born March 26, 1784, at Norwich; Gurdon, born Nov. 5, 1788, at Franklin, married Anna Morgan; Abigail, born April 21, 1769, at Norwich, married Jabez Williams.

Isaiah Abel, born at Norwich, Conn., July 24, 1738, youngest son of Benjamin Abel and Lydia Hazen, of Norwich, was a great grand-son of John Post and Hester Hyde, of Norwich. He married Nov. 5, 1762, Rhoda Pettis. They settled at Norwich, where they had five children recorded to them. Those children were: Azel, born July 9, 1763, at Norwich; Wyllys, born June 11, 1777, at Norwich; a child, born March 24, 1769, at Norwich, died unnamed; Lucretia, born Nov. 28, 1765, at Norwich; Rhoda, born May 15, 1772, at Norwich.

Hannah Abel, born at Norwich, Conn., March 26, 1727, youngest daughter of Benjamin Abel and Lydia Hazen, of Norwich, was a great grand-daughter of John Post and Hester Hyde, of Norwich. She married Jan. 11, 1749, Deacon Simeon Lathrop, born Jan. 15, 1723, at Norwich, youngest son of Irael Lathrop and Mary Fellows, of Norwich. They settled at the New Concord or Bozrah Society in Norwich, where she died Sept. 17,

1802. Their children were: Simeon, born Aug. 4, 1753, at Norwich, married Elizabeth Calkins; Roger, born Dec. 3, 1754, at Norwich; Oliver, born Sept. 9, 1756, at Norwich, married Dec. 13, 1781, his third cousin, Eunice Hough, fourth daughter of Capt. David Hough and his first wife, Desire Clark. They removed to Hartland, Vt., and had a family: Zabdiel, born Nov. 30, 1762, at Noswich, married first, Margaret Tracy, second, Abigail Harris; Andrew, born Oct. 26, 1764, at Norwich, married first, Lucretia Smith, second, Zerviah Polley; Hannah, born Aug. 28, 1749, at Norwich, probably married July 9, 1769, Christopher Calkins; Eunice' born Aug. 17, 1751, at Norwich, probably married Oct. 29, 1772, Stephen Woodward, at Bozrah; Lydia born Sept. 2, 1758, at Norwich, probably married John Fish; Sarah, born Sept. 22, 1760, at Norwich.

Joseph Tracy, born at Norwich, Conn., Oct. 17, 1706, eldest son of Capt. Joseph Tracy and Mary Abel, of Norwich, was a great grand-son of John Post and Hoster Hyde, of the second generation. He married Nov. 5, 1739, Anna Hinckley, born Oct. 5, 1716, at Lebanon, third daughter of Gershom Hinckley and Mary Buel, of Lebanon. They settled at Norwich, where he held the office of constable and collector for nearly thirty years. She died Jan. 8, 1801, aged 84, and he died April 19, 1787. Their children were: Jarred, born Oct. 10, 1741, at Norwich, married Margaret Grant.

Frederick, born Aug. 3, 1749, at Norwich, married Deborah Thomas, his fourth cousin of the Tracy blood, and third cousin of his father, of the Hyde blood, eldest daughter of Ebenezer Thomas, of Norwich, by his second wife, Deborah Hyde.

Uriah Tracy, born Aug. 9, 1753, at Norwich, married Feb. 9, 1794, Lydia Hallam, of New London, [the lady who was engaged to be married to the unfortunate Capt. Hale, of the army of the revolution, who was taken and executed by the British as a spy.) They settled at Norwich, where he was a merchant, and died in 1832. They had one son, William George, born May 11, 1787, died Oct. 31, 1834, s. p.

Ruby, born May 14, 1746, at Norwich, and died July 9, 1751.

Anna, born Nov. 30, 1751, at Norwich, resided there and died in 1825, unmarried.

Lois, born Aug. 19, 1755, at Norwich, resided there and died in 1825, unmarried.

Dr. Elisha Tracy, born at Norwich, Conn., May 17, 1712, second son of Capt. Joseph Tracy and Mary Abel, of Norwich, was a great grand-son of John Post and Hester Hyde, of the second generation. He graduated at Yale in 1738, and was a distinguished physician and surgeon. He married June 16, 1743 Lucy Huntington, born May 32, 1722, at Norwich, daughter of Deacon Ebenezer Huntington and Sarah Leffingwell, and granddaughter of Deacon Simon Huntington, the second, and Lydia Gager, of Norwich. They settled at Norwich, where he was distinguished for his classical attainments, as well as for his professional skill and for his moral and social qualities. She died Oct. 12, 1751, at Norwich. His children by her were: Lucy, born July 20, 1744, at Norwich, married Dr. Philip Turner; Alice, born Oct. 11, 1745, at Norwich, married Elisha Leffingwell; Lucretia, born Sept. 5, 1747, at Norwich, lived there and died March 28, 1825, unmarried; Lydia, born Dec. 26, 1749, at Norwich, married Alvan Fosdick, of Boston, had three sons and one daughter: Phinehas G., Gregory, John, Mary or Lydia. He died. She survived him and died in 1825, at Norwich.

Philura, born Sept. 30, 1751, at Norwich, married Samuel Huntington. After the death of his first wife, he married April 16, 1754, his third cousin, Elizabeth Dorr, born April 16, 1735, at Lyme, Conn., third daughter of Edmund Dorr and Mary Griswold, of Lyme. She died March 23, 1781, at Norwich. He then married Oct. 19, 1781, Lois (Hinckley) Huntington, widow of Nehemiah Huntington, Esq., of Bozrah, but had no issue by her. He died May 1, 1783, at Norwich, and she died Oct. 3, 1790. His children by his second wife were: Phinehas L., born June 29, 1755, at Norwich, was a soldier of the revolution, and died in the army at Roxbury, aged 20 years.

Philemon, born May 30, 1757, at Norwich, married Abigail Trott.

Elisha, born May 27, 1766, at Norwich, married Lucy Coit Huntington.

Joseph Winslow, born Aug. 11, 1769, at Norwich, died Feb. 6, 1770.

Elizabeth, born June 29, 1760, at Norwich, died Oct. 30, 1773.

Charlotte, born May 27, 1762, at Norwich, resided there and died in 1820, unmarried.

Mary, born May 3, 1764, at Norwich, resided there and died in 1858, unmarried.

Deborah Dorr, born Nov. 9, 1770, at Norwich, resided there and died in 1824, unmarried.

Margaret Tracy, born at Norwich, Conn., May 11, 1710, second daughter of Capt. Joseph Tracy and Mary Abel, of Norwich, was a great grand-daughter of John Post and Hester Hyde, of the second generation. She married Sept. 23, 1733, her second cousin of the Tracy blood, William Waterman, born July 20, 1710, at Norwich, eldest son of John Waterman, of Norwich, by his second wife, Judith Woodward. [This John Waterman, born March, 1672, second son of Ensign Thomas Waterman, first, of Norwich, and Miriam Tracy. John Waterman's first wife was Elizabeth Lathrop, by whom he had two sons and two daughters: Eleazer, who married Martha Adgate; John, who died unmarried; Elizabeth, who probably died young; Hannah, (this Hannah was grand-daughter of John Waterman and Miriam Tracy) whose first husband was Absalom King, of Long Island, and who afterwards married Benedict Arnold, of Norwich, and was mother of Gen. Benedict Arnold, the traitor, who was born Jan. 3, 1741, at Norwich. John Waterman, by his second wife, Judith Woodward, had four children: William, Samuel, Ebenezer and Peter. By his third wife, Elizabeth Basset, who he married in 1721, he had three more: Mary, David Basset and Elizabeth.] William Waterman and his wife settled at Norwich, where she died June 4, 1767, and where he died Nov. 7, 1789. Their children were: William, born March 17, 1748, at Norwich.

Judith, born March 20, 1736, at Norwich, married March 18, 1762, Beriah Bill, of Norwich, and had two children recorded to them at Norwich: Judith, born March 13, 1763; Uriah, born March 1, 1765.

Abigail, born March 12, 1739, at Norwich, married Jan. 15, 1783, her fourth cousin of the Hyde blood, Marshfield Parsons, eldest son of the Rev. Jonathan Parsons and Phebe Griswold, of Lyme, died March 14, 1793, at Lyme, s. p.

Lydia, born Sept. 13, 1741, at Norwich, probably married Jesse Birchard, of Bozrah, and had a daughter, Mary, and probably other children.

Margaret, born March 24, 1744, at Norwich.

Mary, born Sept. 7, 1746, at Norwich, probably married Oct. 20, 1881, Joseph Perkins.

Irene Tracy, born at Norwich, Conn., Jan. 15, 1719, fifth daughter of Capt. Joseph Tracy and Mary Abel, of Norwich, was a great grand-daughter of John Post and Hester Hyde, of the second generation. She married Dec. 20, 1743, Daniel Burnham, born March 21, 1718, at Norwich, eldest son of Eleazer Burnham and Lydia Waterman, grand-son of Thomas Waterman, the first, and Miriam Tracy, of Norwich. They settled at Norwich, where they had four children recorded to them: Zacharias, born June 26, 1747, at Norwich; Elias, born June 17, 1754 at Norwich; Irene, born Nov. 18, 1744, at Norwich, married Aaron Bushnell; Abigail, born May 29, 1752, at Norwich, died July 10, 1756.

Christopher Huntington, born at Norwich, Conn., June 20, 1719, eldest son of Christopher Huntington, of Norwich, by his first wife, Abigail (Abel) Lathrop, was a great grand-son of John Post and Hester Hyde, of the second generation. He married Sept. 19, 1748, Sarah Bingham, of Norwich. He was a physician and was deacon and clerk of the New Concord Society church.

He died March, 1800, at Bozrah. Their children were: Christopher, born July 14, 1749, at Norwich, died Feb. 11, 1759.

Thomas, born Oct. 28, 1757, at Norwich, married first, Abigail Backus, second, —— Griswold.

Second Christopher, born March 31, 1766, at Norwich, married Lucy Culver.

Sarah, born Jan. 28, 1751, at Norwich, lived in Bozrah, and died unmarried.

Abigail, born June 13, 1753, at Norwich, married April 3, 1778, Job Talcott, of Bolton, Conn

Ruth, born Aug. 14, 1755, at Norwich, married Sept. 22, 1775, Rev. Thomas Baldwin, D. D., born Dec. 23, 1753, at Norwich. They settled at Canaan, N. H., where he became a Baptist clergyman. She died Feb. 11, 1812, and had six children, only two of whom survived her. He then married Margaret Duncan, of Haverhill, N. H., and became a distinguished clergyman at Boston. One of his daughters married —— Holt.

Elisha Huntington, born at Norwich, Conn., Sept. 22, 1720, second son of Christopher Huntington, of Norwich, by his first wife, Abigail (Abel) Lathrop, was a great grand-son of John Post and Hester Hyde, of the second generation. He married Dec. 31, 1760, Dinah Chapman, of New London, born July 20, 1734. They settled at Norwich, where he died Feb. 12, 1765. Their children were: Elisha, born April 23, 1765, at Norwich, married Nancy Rude; Dinah, born Feb. 13, 1765, at Norwich, married May 19, 1786, Samuel Judd.

Barnabas Huntington, born at Norwich, Conn., May 29, 1728, fifth son of Christopher Huntington, of Norwich, by his first wife, Abigail (Abel) Lathrop, was a great grand-son of John Post and Hester Hyde, of the third generation. He married Dec. 11, 1751, Anne Wright, of Hebron. They settled at Norwich, West Farms, now Franklin, where he was deacon of the church, and one of its prominent citizens.

Zabdiel Lathrop, born at Norwich, Conn., Nov. 30, 1762, fourth son of Deacon Simeon Lathrop and Hannah Abel, was a great grand-son of Margaret Post, of the third generation. He married Sept. 22, 1783, Margaret Tracy, the third, who died Oct. 4, 1783, s. p. He then married June 6, 1785, Abigail Harris, of Lebanon. They settled at Bozrah, where they had three children recorded to them: Alfred, born Nov. 5, 1786, at Bozrah; Zabdiel, born June 2, 1791, at Bozrah; Caroline, born Sept. 2, 1788, at Bozrah.

Andrew Lathrop, born at Norwich, Conn., Oct. 26, 1764, fifth son of Deacon Simeon Lathrop and Hannah Abel, was a great grand-son of Margaret Post, of the third generation. He probably married Jan. 22, 1789, Lucretia Smith, of Franklin. They settled at Bozrah, where he was a Justice of the Peace. She died Oct. 9, 1801. His children by her were: Simeon, born Nov. 25, 1792, at Bozrah, probably married Abigail ———, who died, and had by her one child, William, born April 17, 1817, at Bozrah. He then married Dec. 20, 1820, Phebe Peckham, of Franklin, born about 1800. They settled at Bozrah, where she died Aug. 11, 1847, and where they had eight children recorded to them: Andrew, born March 10, 1822; Lucy, born May 22, 1823; Jabez Smith, born May 28, 1824; Alanson Peckham, born July 21, 1826; Jane, born Oct. 25, 1828; Daniel Austin and Lydia Zerviah, (twins) born April 23, 1832, and Anne, born May 20, 1834.

Azariah, born Feb. 25, 1796, at Bozrah, married Dec. 2, 1824, Talitha Huntington, born Feb. 13, 1794, at Franklin, third daughter of Elisha Huntington and Nancy Rude, of Franklin. They settled at Franklin, and removed to Vernon, and had five children: Azariah Willes, born April 24, 1826, at Franklin. He was a lawyer, and went to Iowa: Elisha Huntington, born Aug. 27, 1827, at Franklin; Philena Maria, born April 26, 1829, and died July 11, 1831, at Franklin; Eliza L., born November, 1831; Nancy Huntington, born Oct. 3, 1835; Dice, born Dec. 3, 1789, at Bozrah; Philena, born April 10, 1791, at Bozrah; Apame, born July 25, 1794, at Bozrah; Lucy, born March 8, 1798, at Bozrah; Eunice, born June 14, 1799, at Bozrah. Andrew Lathrop, Esq., then married May 30, 1802, Zerviah Polley, of Bozrah, where he probably died.

Lydia Lathrop, born at Norwich, Conn., Sept. 2, 1758, third daughter of Deacon Simeon Lathrop and Hannah Abel, was a great grand-daughter of Margaret Post, of the third generation. She married April 2, 1786, John Fish, of Bozrah, where they settled, and had six children recorded to them: Simeon, born Feb. 1, 1787, at Bozrah; John, born Sept. 25, 1788, at Bozrah; Miller, born June 5, 1791, at Bozrah; Electa, born April 23, 1793, at Bozrah; Lydia, born Aug. 6, 1796, at Bozrah; Margaret, born Nov. 17, 1799, at Bozrah.

Jared Tracy, born at Norwich, Conn., Oct. 10, 1741, eldest son of Capt. Joseph Tracy and Anne Hinckley, of Norwich, was a great grand-son of Margaret Post, of the third generation. He married Oct. 20, 1765, Margaret Grant, of Norwich, where they settled. He was a justice of the peace, and was a commissary of supplies for the American army, during the siege of Boston. He also had Gen. Burgoine's army under his charge after their surrender at Saratoga. He was a member of the legislature. He was a merchant and a ship-master. He died Dec. 25, 1790, at Martinique, W. I. Their children were: William Gidney, born Nov. 15, 1768, at Norwich, married Jan. 19, 1800, Rachel Huntington, born April 4, 1779, at Norwich, daughter of Judge Benjamin Huntington and Anna Huntington, and maternally grand-daughter of Col. Jabez Huntington, of Windham, and his second wife, the widow Sarah Wetmore, (see Goodwin, 54, note.) They settled at Whitesboro', N. Y., where he died April 15, 1830. She died April 7, 1852, at Utica. They had nine children born at Whitesboro': Susanna, born Nov. 20, 1800, married November, 1834, Moses Bagg, of Utica, and died July 17, 1859, while on a visit to Saratoga Springs. Margaret, born Jan. 18, 1803, married April, 1830, Rev. Chauncey E. Goodrich, of Utica, N. Y., and had four children: Anne, born May, 1831; Cornelia, born in 1833; Susan, born in 1836, and Rachel, born in 1839. William, born June 16, 1805, graduated at Union college in 1824, and was a prominent and successful lawyer. He married May 20, 1831, Lucy Perkins, daughter of Frederich Perkins, of Lisbon, Conn. They settled at Utica, and removed to New York, where they were living in 1859, and had three children: Lucy Eldridge, born May 5, 1835, married May 22, 1861, William P. Lee, of New York; Catherine Parker, born Dec. 8, 1839; and William Frederick, born June 15, 1837, died Feb. 11, 1839. Anne Huntington, born Oct. 7, 1807, married May 1, 1831, William Curtis Noyes, a lawyer, and settled at Whitesboro', where she died Oct. 5, 1838, had one child, Rachel Tracy, born April 1, 1832. He removed to New York, and married a daughter of Frederick A. Talmadge, and was living at New York in 1860, and was one of the most distinguished lawyers of that city. Charles, born Feb. 17, 1810, graduated at Yale in 1832, and was a lawyer. He married Aug. 30, 1837, Louisa Kirkland, daughter of Gen. Joseph Kirkland, of Utica. They settled at Utica, and removed to New York, where they were living in 1859, and had five children: Anne Huntington, born June 10, 1838; Mary Kirkland, born Nov. 23, 1839; Frances Louisa, born May 15, 1842; Clara, born Oct. 30, 1843, and Charles Edward. Catherine, born July 10, 1812, married Oct. 17, 1834, Milton D. Parker, of Utica, who died Dec. 8, 1839. She was lost by the wrecking of the steamboat Swallow, in April, 1845, near Athens, N. Y. They had two children: Charlotte Huntington, born Oct. 22, 1835, and Catherine Roxanna, born June 5, 1839. Henry, born Feb. 10, 1815, was a civil engineer, and died May 31, 1851, at Panama, N. G., unmarried. Edward Huntington, born March 31, 1817, was a civil engineer, unmarried in 1858. Frances, born Jan. 6, 1821, married March 16, 1852, William Henry Welles, of Brattleboro', Vt., son of Ebenezer Welles and Mary Chester. He was through his mother, descended from Mabel Harlakenden, and from the kings and nobility of England. They were living in New York in 1862, and had one daughter, Julia Chester, born in 1856.

  Joseph Winslow, born March 9, 1773, at Norwich, married

Sept. 21, 1807, Wealthy Huntington, born Jan. 8, 1780, at Norwich, daughter of Elijah Huntington, Esq., of Bozrah, by his second wife, Lydia Baldwin. They settled at Norwich, and he died April 3, 1845, and she died July 11, 1849. They had six children, born at Norwich: Jarred Winslow, born May 29, 1812, a merchant in New York in 1859; James Joseph, born Dec. 3, 1814, a merchant in New York in 1859; Edward Huntington, born April 21, 1817, married Jan. 10, 1856, Louisa H. Thomas, of the state of Delaware, was a merchant, and they were living at New York in 1859; Sarah Grant, born Aug. 21, 1819, died in 1838, unmarried; Cornelia Margaret, born Oct. 15, 1822, living at Norwich in 1857, unmarried; Lydia Huntington, living at Norwich in 1857, unmarried.

Gardiner, born Feb. 23, 1777, at Norwich, married Feb. 9, 1805, Catherine Lansing, daughter of Cornelius Lansing, of Lansingburgh, N. Y., where they settled, and where he was for many years the proprietor and publisher of the "Lansingburgh Gazette. They subsequently removed to Utica, N. Y. They had six children, born at Lansingburgh: Cornelius Lansing, born Nov. 25, 1805, graduated at Union College in 1824, and was a lawyer; he married Sept. 9, 1845, at Cohoes, Mary Olmstead, born Aug. 1, 1808, at Onondaga, N. Y., daughter of George W. Olmstead and Mary Tyler. They settled at Lansingburg, and in May, 1846, removed to Troy, N. Y., where they lived in 1863. They had three children, born at Troy: Cornelius Lansing, born Feb. 2, 1848, died Dec. 17, 1856; Mary Elizabeth, born May 2, 1850, and Catherine, born Feb. 6, 1852, died Feb. 20, 1854. George, born Nov. 30, 1812, married at Utica, Sept. 28, 1836, Carline Drake Tracy, daughter of Seymour Tracy, of Franklin, Conn., maternally a lineal descendant of George Drake, the brother and heir of Sir Francis Drake, the great captain of Queen Elizabeth, (Sir Francis Drake died unmarried,) she was also great niece of John Fitch, one of the originators of the steamboat; her grand-father, Uriah Tracy, fell in the battle of Lundy's Lane, and was buried under one of the church windows there. They settled at Utica, N. Y., and removed to Milwaukee, Wis., in June, 1856, and had two children: Olive, born July 11, 1837, and George Lansing, born March 25, 1841. Catherine Margaret, born Jan. 17, 1816, married at Utica, Sept. 6, 1836, John E. Lyon, of Cleveland, O., where they settled, and removed to Oswego, N. Y., and had four children: Catherine Tracy, born Sept. 14, 1838; James, born Aug. 2, 1841; Gardiner Tracy, born Dec. 9, 1847, and Annie, born April 10, 1850. Susan Hester, born Feb. 23, 1818, married at Utica, Feb. 10, 1847, Ashbel H. Barney, of Cleveland, O., and had three children: Gardiner Tracy, born December, 1849, died July 29, 1856; Helen Tracy, born May 16, 1852, and Charles Tracy, born Jan. 27, 1854. They settled in Cleveland, and removed to New York city. James Jared, born Dec. 3, 1819, married at Fortress Monroe, Va., April 25, 1883, Jane Allyn Foote, daughter of George Foote, of Detroit, Mich. They settled at Cleveland, O., and had two children: James Jared, Jr., born Feb. 27, 1884, and Catherine Lansing, born Feb. 27, 1888. Helen Alvord, born Aug. 4, 1823, married at Utica, July 6, 1847, John E. Taylor, of Lansingburgh, N. Y., who graduated at Union college in 1839, and was a lawyer. They had no children. They settled at Troy, N. Y., and removed to Cleveland, O., where he died.

James Grant, born March 16, 1781, at Norwich, married Nov. 30, 1836, Sarah Osgood, born at Andover, Mass. They settled at Syracuse, N. Y., and had three or more children: James Grant, born Oct. 4, 1837; Osgood Vose, born June 25, 1840; William Gardiner, born April 7, 1843, an officer of volunteers in 1863.

Sarah, born Feb. 10, 1767, at Norwich, who died in 1838, unmarried.

Susanna, born Aug. 8, 1770, at Norwich, married March 20, 1795, Gurdon Huntington, born March 16, 1768, at Norwich, son of Judge Benjamin Huntington and Anne Huntington, of Norwich, and afterwards of Rome, N. Y. He was a merchant, and they settled at Norwich, where she died Aug. 21, 1793. He had by her one child, Edward, born Dec. 5, 1792, graduated at Union college in 1810, and was a lawyer. He died Dec. 16, 1816, at New York, unmarried. Gurdon Huntington then married July 6, 1794, Anne Perkins, and lived at Rome, and afterwards New York, and had by her four other children, three of whom died unmarried. The other one, Susanna, married Major James S. Dalliba, of the U. S. army.

Margaret, born July 28, 1782, at Norwich, and died Aug. 1, 1782.

Second Margaret, born Dec. 19, 1783, at Norwich, died Nov. 24, 1786. After the death of Jarred Tracy, his widow married Oct. 30, 1796, Jabez Backus, Esq., of Norwich, and died Nov. 13, 1815.

Lucy Tracy, born at Norwich, Conn., July 20, 1744, eldest daughter of Dr. Elisha Tracy, of Norwich, by his first wife, Lucy Huntington, was a great grand-daughter of Margaret Post, of the third generation. She married April 7, 1763, Dr. Philip Turner, born Feb. 25, 1740, at Norwich, eldest son of Capt. Philip Turner and Mrs. Anne (Huntington) Adgate, of Norwich. [This Anne Huntington Adgate, born March 20, 1715, at Norwich, married April 24, 1739, Capt. Philip Turner, was the widow of Thomas Adgate, the third, of Norwich, and was the third daughter of Daniel Huntington and Abigail Bingham, and grand-daughter of Deacon Simon Huntington, the first, and Sarah Clark, of Norwich. Capt. Philip Turner, born about 1716, at Scituate, was probably a great grand-son of Humphrey Turner, of Scituote, who came from England previous to 1630, as follows: the emigrant, Humphrey Turner, had two sons, named John. The first married Nov. 12, 1645, Mary Brewster. The last, called by his father, young John, married April 25, 1649, Anne James, and had a son, Philip, born Aug. 18, 1672, at Scituate, who was probably the father of Capt. Philip Turner, of Norwich, who died Jan. 13, 1755, in the 39th year of his age.] Dr. Turner, for three years previous to his marriage, had been an assistant surgeon to a provincial regiment, in the service of the Crown, in the French war, and became a very skillful surgeon. They settled at Norwich, where he went into the practice of his profession with distinguished success. At the commencement of the revolution he was with the American troops at Boston. He was with the army at New York in 1776, where his services were of immense value to the wounded in the battles of Flatbash, Harlem Heights and White Plains. In 1777 he was appointed surgeon-general of the army of the United States for the eastern department; the duties of which situation he continued to discharge with ability to about the close of the war. He then returned to his private practice at Norwich, which he continued there for nearly twenty years. About 1800 they removed to the city of New York. He was soon after appointed post-surgeon to the troops in the several fortifications in and about New York. It was there that, in the spring of 1809, the writer hereof, while visiting a brother, who was an officer in the army on Bedlow's Island, became acquainted with the then venerable Dr. Turner, (whose wife was a first cousin of the writer's mother.) He died in 1815, at New York, and was burried with military honors. Their children were: John, born May 29, 1764, at Norwich, married Hannah Huntington, born April 29, 1765, daughter of Jonathan Huntington and Eunice Lathrop, and settled at Norwich, where he was an eminent physician and surgeon, and was a member of the legislature. He died May 7, 1837, at Norwich, and she died May 7, 1845. They had four children: George Frederick, born about 1791, died Feb. 9, 1813, at Norwich, died unmarried; Charles W., born about 1793, died Feb. 13, 1794; Julia Frances Marionette, married Rev. George Perkins, and died leaving a daughter, Hannah Parkins, who died unmarried; Elizabeth H., the second wife of Rev. George Perkins, had by him two sons: John Turner Perkins, died unmarried; George Turner Perkins, who in 1859, was the sole surviving descendent of Dr. John Turner.

William Pitt, born Sept. 3, 1766, at Norwich, the poet and satirist. He married Phebe ———, and settled at New York, where he was a physician, and was in the service of the United

States as an assistant surgeon. They had four children: George F., died s. p.; Francis Lathrop; Marvin Waite; Marionette. The three last were living in 1859.

Lucy Ann, born at Norwich, married Dr. Gurdon Lathrop, born Dec. 6, 1767, at Norwich, eldest son of Azariah Lathrop and Abigail Huntington, of Norwich, and grand-son of Nathaniel Lathrop and Anne Backus, of Norwich, and great grand-son of Samuel Lathrop and Hannah Adgate, of Norwich. He graduated at Yale in 1787, and was a physician. He died in 1828. They had two children: John, who was a merchant in Savannah, Ga., died unmarried; Abby Maria, married Edward Whiting, of Norwich, died s. p.

Nancy, born April 1, 1772, at Norwich, married Nov. 15, 1810, Judge Marvin Waite, of New London, born Dec. 16, 1746, at Lyme, second son of Richard Waite, of Lyme, by his first wife, Elizabeth Marvin. She was his third wife, and they settled at New London. Judge Marvin Waite was a lawyer, and went into practice at New London about 1769, in partnership with Samuel Holden Parsons, and was a successful practitioner there until he retired from the bar about 1800. He was frequently a member of the legislature, was a judge of the county court, was a presidential elector at the first election of Gen. Washington, and was one of the council appointed to dispose of the lands belonging to the state and establish the school fund. He died June, 1815, at New London, and his last wife died Apri., 1851, at Norwich. He had by her one child, John Turner Waite, born Aug. 27, 1811, at New London. He was educated at Trinity college, Hartford, and was a lawyer. He married April, 1842, Elizabeth Harris, at New York. They settled at Norwich Town, where he held the office of post-master for a few years, and where he was a successful and very distinguished lawyer, and where they were living in 1863. They had three children: Marvin, born in 1843; Anne Eliza, born in 1846; and Mary Elizabeth, born in 1856. Marvin was a lieutenant of volunteers, and was killed at the battle of Antietam, Sept. 17, 1862. The first wife of Judge Marvin Waite, to whom he was married April 25, 1779, was Martha Jones, of New London, by whom he had seven children: Marvin; Martha Jones; Harriet, who married Francis Richards; Richard; Howard; Oliver, and Eliza, married Jedediah Huntington, of Norwich. He then married April 22, 1805, the widow Harriet Saltonstall, and had by her one child, second Marvin, born Dec. 10, 1806.

Elizabeth Tracy born at Norwich, married Aug. 14, 1793, Daniel Lathrop, born Oct. 13, 1769, at Norwich, youngest son of Dr. Joshua Lathrop, of Norwich, by his second wife, Mercy Eells, of Stonington. [This Dr. Joshua Lathrop, born May 8, 1723, at Norwich, graduated at Yale in 1743, and was a physician and druggist, married May 21, 1748, Hannah Gardner, who died July 24, 1750, s. p., and after her death, married Nov. 5, 1761, Mercy Eells, of Stonington, and died Oct. 29, 1807, was the youngest son of Thomas Lathrop and Lydia Abel, and grand-son of Samuel Lathrop, the second, and Hannah Adgate, of Norwich.] Daniel Lathrop graduated at Yale in 1787. They settled at Norwich, where he died in 1825. They had four children, born at Norwich: Jane Eliza, born July, 26, 1795, married Jonathan George Washington Trumbull, son of David Trumbull and Sarah Backus, and grand-son of the first Gov. Jonathan Trumbull and Faith Robinson, of Lebanon. He graduated at Yale in 1807, and was a lawyer. They settled at Norwich, where he died in 1853, and where she also died. They had a son Daniel Lathrop Trumbull, and perhaps other children: Frank Turner, born Aug. 9, 1798; Ann Matilda, born March 10, 1800, died unmarried; Cornelia Sophia, born July 30, 1804, married George G. Willes, and died leaving a son, William Henry Willes, who was living in 1859, unmarried.

Sophia, born at Norwich, married Judge Alexander Richards of New London, afterwards of St. Lawrence county, N. Y. He was a judge of the county court, collector of customs for the district of Oswegatchie. She died s. p.

Alice Tracy, born at Norwich, Conn., Oct. 11, 1745, second daughter of Dr. Elisha Tracy, of Norwich, by his first wife, Lucy Huntington, was a great grand-daughter of Margaret Post, of the third generation. She married June 15, 1766, Elisha Leffingwell, born Nov. 4, 1743, at Norwich, seventh son of Benajah Leffingwell and Joanna Christophers. [This Joanna Christophers, born March 19, 1707, at New London, married Aug. 24, 1726, Benajah Leffingwell, of Norwich, youngest daughter of Judge Richard Christophers, of New London, by his second wife, Grace Turner, of Scituate, Mass., which Richard Christophers, born July 13, 1652, in Devonshire, son of Christopher Christophers and Mary, his wife, who came to New London in 1665. Grace Turner was a daughter of John Turner and Mary Brewster, of Scituate, and grand-daughter of Jonathan Brewster and Lucretia, his wife, of Duxbury, afterwards of New London, and great grand-daughter of elder William Brewster, of the Mayflower. The wife of Jonathan Brewster, with his son William, came over with Elder Brewster, in the Mayflower. But Jonathan, the husband, came over in the Little Ann, Nov. 10, 1621. This Benajah Leffingwell, born Aug. 9, 1693, at Norwich, married Aug. 24, 1726, Joanna Christophers, and had eight sons and five daughters, was the third son of Thomas Leffingwell and Mary Bushnell, and grand-son of Lieut. Thomas Leffingwell the first, of Norwich, and Mary, his wife, and was also grand-son of Richard Bushnell, of Saybrook, and Mary Marvin.] Elisha Leffingwell and wife settled at Norwich, but I have not ascertained the dates of their deaths. Their children were: Dyar, born April 6, 1767, at Norwich, died Oct. 1770; second Dyar, born Oct. 5, 1770, at Norwich, married his mother's fourth cousin, Hannah Waterman, eldest daughter of Arunah Waterman and Hannah Leffingwell, of Norwich, afterwards of St. Johnsbury, Vt. After her death, he married the widow Eunice (Sutherland) Brewster, and died Dec. 5, 1821.

Elisha, born Feb. 28, 1778, at Norwich, married his mother's fourth cousin, Frances Thomas, the eldest daughter of Simeon

Thomas and Lucretia Deshon, of Norwich, and he was lost at sea.

Martin, born October, 1785, at Norwich, married March, 1819, his mother's fourth cousin, Mary Thomas, eldest daughter of Thomas Langrel Thomas, of Norwich, by his first wife, Eunice Birchard. He died at sea in 1819, s. p., and she was living at Geneva, N. Y., in 1859.

Lucy Huntington, born Sept. 4, 1768, at Norwich, married her second cousin, Deacon Simon Abel, of Bozrah, eldest son of Simeon Abel and Martha Crocker.

Sarah, born Nov. 27, 1772, at Norwich, married Roswell Culver, and died at Buffalo, N. Y. They had three children: Jonathan E., married Miss Denison, (sister of Rev. Charles Denison) who was a grocer at Norwich, and removed to Wisconsin; Asa, who lived at New York, and afterwards went to New Orleans: Cornelia, married ―――― Crandall, a merchant of Norwich, and afterwards of Buffalo.

Alice, born Aug. 8, 1775, at Norwich, married her second cousin of the Tracy blood, and her mother's fourth cousin of the Hyde blood, Henry Tracy, eldest son of Capt. Frederick Tracy and Deborah Thomas, of Norwich.

Nancy, born Feb. 15, 1781, at Norwich, married Sept. 8, 1814, Deacon Nehemiah Huntington, born April 20, 1782, at Norwich, youngest son of Elijah Huntington, of Bozrah, by his second wife, Lydia Baldwin, and grand-son of Isaac Huntington and Rebecca Lathrop. [That Isaac Huntington, born Feb. 5, 1688, at Norwich, married Feb. 31, 1716, Rebecca Lathrop, born April 20, 1695, at Norwich, eldest daughter of Israel Lathrop and Rebecca Bliss, of Norwich, was a justice of the peace and a member of the legislature, and was town clerk of Norwich for about sixty years. He was the second son of Deacon Christopher Huntington, born Nov. 1, 1660, at Norwich, and his first wife, Sarah Adgate.] Deacon Nehemiah Huntington and wife settled at Bozrah, where she died July 12, 1835. He had by her four children, born at Bozrah: Nancy Leffingwell, born June 14,

1815, married Oct. 24, 1841, Alba C. Thompson, a merchant of Norwich, where they were living in 1858, and had five children: Elizabeth Huntington, born Aug. 19, 1842; Malvina Huntington, born May 11, 1845; Frank, born July 23, 1848, died in infancy; Annie, born Aug. 30, 1849; and Caroline Hamlin, born March 5, 1855. Elijah Baldwin, born Aug. 14, 1816, educated at Yale, married March 6, 1843, Julia Welch, daughter of Thomas Welch and Laura Lathrop, of Windham. He was a clergyman, and was settled in Putnam, Conn., in 1848, and from 1850 he was engaged in teaching. He received the honorary degree of Master of Arts at Yale, in 1851. In 1861 they were living at Stamford, Conn., where he was principal of a select school. He was then engaged in preparing a genealogical history of the Huntington family. They had five children: Abby Swift, born April 7, 1845, died Feb. 12, 1846; Julia Swift, born Sept. 1, 1846; Clara Louisa, born July 27, 1848; Sarah Lee, born Sept. 12, 1850, died Dec. 24, 1850; and Edmund Clement, born May 30, 1852, died Sept. 9, 1852.

Elisha Tracy, born Dec. 28, 1817, married Sept. 2, 1844, Malvina Boswell, daughter of Dr. Thomas Boswell, of Norwich City. He was a gold-smith at Norwich, and died Feb. 16, 1859, at Norwich, s. p., where she was living in 1861.

William Dyar, born Dec. 18, 1821, married Nov. 16, 1847, Mary Anne Kinney, daughter of Thomas Kinney, of Norwich. She died July 27, 1848. He then married May 19, 1852, Calista Reed born March 29, 1830, daughter of James Reed, Esq., of Springfield, N. Y. They were living at Providence in 1860. He had one child by his first wife, William Tracy, born July 16, 1848, and one by his last wife, Mary Anne, born May 28, 1855. After the death of his first wife, Deacon Nehemiah Huntington married Dec. 21, 1741, Mrs. Nancy (Hinckley) Hough, widow of Jirah Isham Hough, and daughter of Timothy Hinckley and Saloma Strong, of Lebanon. He died June 2, 1852, at Bozrah, where she was living in 1858, s. p.

Lucretia, born Nov. 14, 1782, at Norwich, married Dec. 25, 1803, Elijah Huntington, born Dec. 19, 1777, at Norwich, brother of her sister Nancy's husband, and second son of Elijah Huntington, Esq., by his second wife, Lydia Baldwin. They settled at Bozrah, where he was a farmer and a justice of the peace, and where she died Oct. 30, 1816. He had by her three children, born at Bozrah: Philura Leffingwell, born March 23, 1805, marriad March 22, 1832, Christopher Leffingwell Lathrop, son of Deacon Charles Lathrop, of Norwich. They removed to Cleveland, O., where she died Aug. 13, 1843, leaving one daughter, Elizabeth Hutchins, born Feb. 8, 1836, married in 1860, William Merriam, of Cleveland. Winslow Tracy, born Aug. 25, 1807, married June 1, 1830, Almira Carson, of Pittsfield, Mass. He graduated at Pittsfield medical school in 1829, and was a physician. They lived at Ohio City, where she died February, 1838. He then married July 12, 1840, at Akron, O., Julia (Swift) Babcock, daughter of Chief Justice Zepheniah Swift, of Windham, Conn. They settled at Akron, where he died Dec. 23, 1849, from a wound received in conducting a post-mortem examination. He had five children: William Henry, born June 12, 1832, married Kate Stanley; Frances Elizabeth, born July 30, 1834; Cornelia Winslow, born Aug. 3, 1837, married in 1861, William Silliman Huntington, of Cleveland; Julia Almira, born Aug. 6, 1845, and Emely Lucretia, born Aug. 12, 1849. Caroline Matilda, born Sept. 29, 1809, married Sept. 16, 1835, Samuel K. Hamlin, Esq., of Buffalo, where they were living in 1858, and had two children: Charles W., born in 1836, and Harriet Cornelia, born in 1842. Elijah Huntington then married June 13, 1821, Olive Starke, born March 17, 1797, at Bozrah, fourth daughter of Joshua Starke and Olive Lathrop, of Bozrah, where he was living in 1863. She died Sept. 26, 1862. He had by her three other children, born at Bozrah: Lucretia Leffingwell, born Sept. 18, 1822, married March 7, 1853, her first cousin, Lemuel Barlow Starke, born July 1, 1823, eldest son of Dr. Joshua Starke and Silence Rose, of Granville, O., where she died May 13, 1856, and had two children. Albert Elijah, born Aug. 4, 1828, a farmer, living at Bozrah in 1852, unmarried. Albert Joshua, born June 11, 1834, a soldier in the Union army in 1862, unmarried.

Philena, born in October, 1791, at Norwich. She died unmarried.

Philura Tracy, born at Norwich, Conn., Sept. 30, 1751, fifth daughter of Dr. Elisha Tracy, ef Norwich, by his first wife, Lucy Huntington, was a great grand-daughter of Margaret Post of the third generation. She married Dec. 19, 1782, her third cousin of the Tracy blood, Samuel Huntington, born Nov. 15, 1751, at Norwich, son of Rev. Simon Huntington and Hannah Tracy, of Norwich, his first wife. [This Hannah Tracy, born Sept. 2, 1727 at Norwich, married Rev. Simon Huntington, was the second daughter of Daniel Tracy and Abigail Leffingwell, and granddaughter of Daniel Tracy, the first, of Norwich, and his first wife, Abigail Adgate. Rev. Simon Huntington, born Sept. 12, 1719, graduated at Yale in 1741, and died Oct. 2, 1801, a son of Ebenezer Huntington and Sarah Leffingwell, and grand-son of Deacon Simon Huntington, the second, and Lydia Gager.] He was a farmer, and they settled at Norwich, where he died June 23, 1812, and she died Aug. 30, 1816. Their children were: Roger born Feb. 1, 1784, at Norwich, married Jan. 30, 1814, Anne Denison, born about 1784, daughter of Benadam Denison. He was a merchant, and they settled at Norwich, where she died Sept. 15, 1819. He had by her three children: Harriet Denison, born Jan. 9, 1815, died May 22, 1816; James Denison, born Jan. 25, 1817, was living at Meriden, Conn. in 1857, unmarried; Mary Ann, born March 30, 1819, living with her step-mother in 1857, unmarried. He then married in 1820, Amelia Matilda Lambert, and lived at Norwich, where he was a member of the house of representatives and a senator. He was comptroller of the state of Connecticut. He died June 27, 1852, at Norwich, and she was living in 1858. He had by her five other children: Lydia Lambert, born Nov. 6, 1821, died Feb. 22, 1824; Louis Charles Lambert, born April 26, 1824, married Dec. 20, 1848, Mary L. Tuite, and in 1858 was a salt manufacturer at St. Martins, W. I., and had five children: Eliza Matilda, born Sept. 13, 1850; Caroline Maria, born June 10, 1852; Louis Charles Lambert, born May 28, 1854; James Clement, born April 17, 1857, and Edward Carrol, born June 22, 1859, died Oct. 26, 1760. John Fosdick, born July 27, 1827, died Oct. 23, 1828. Amelia Matilda, born Nov. 15, 1829, married December, 1857, Dr. C. C. Thomas, of Augusta, Ga.; Gilbert Clement, born April 9, 1841, unmarried in 1862.

Gilbert, born May 26, 1796, at Norwich, married June 5, 1826, Mary Anne Clement, died Aug. 21 1841, at Norwich, s. p., where she was living in 1858.

Hannah Tracy, born June 19, 1790, at Norwich, married Nov. 19, 1810, Solomon Dickinson, a farmer of Hatfield, Mass., and had four children: Abby Huntington, born Sept. 8, 1811, unmarried in 1857; Daniel Huntington, born Jan. 28, 1816, living with his father at Hatfield in 1857, unmarried; Philura Tracy, born Jan. 31, 1818, married in 1843, George W. Hubbard, a farmer at Hatfield; Harriet Maria, born Sept. 21, 1825, married in 1849, David F. Wells, of Hartford, and in 1858, had one daughter.

Dr. Philemon Tracy, born at Norwich, Conn., May 30, 1757, second son of Dr. Elisha Tracy, of Norwich, by his second wife, Elizabeth Dorr, was a great grand-son of Margaret Post of the third generation. He married in 1785, Abigail Trott, and settled at Norwich, where he was a very distinguished physician, and received the honorary degree of doctor of medicine at Yale in 1817. He practiced medicine in his native town more than fifty-five years. He excelled in the investigation of chronic diseases, especially those which from their complication, demanded deep research and accurate discrimination. Mrs. Sigourney says: "His habit was minutely to investigate every symptom before prescribing; to require strict obedience to his prescriptions; to regulate diet and regimen, and to give as little medicine as possible." He died in 1837, at Norwich, aged 80 years, having become blind some time before his death. Their children were:

Phinehas Lyman, born Dec. 25, 1786, at Norwich, graduated at Yale in 1806, and was a lawyer, married Harriet Lay, settled at Batavia, N. Y., where he was a member of Congress, and where he was living in 1859, s. p.

Edward Dorr, born March 21, 1794, at Norwich, married Susan Campbell, and was a lawyer. They settled at Macon, Ga. He was a judge of the superior court. She died September, 1834. He then married Aug. 2, 1835, Caroline Campbell, and died at Macon. He had six children; Anne, Philemon, Edward, Matilda, Campbell, Harriet Charlotte.

Richard Proctor, born March 21, 1791, at Norwich, (twin.) He was a physician, and occupied his father's homestead at Norwich, where he was living in 1860, unmarried. He graduated in 1816 at the medical department of Yale college.

Albert Haller, born June 17, 1793, at Norwich, was a lawyer, and settled at Buffalo, where he was elected to congress at the early age of 24, but attained the constitutional age before congress convened in December, 1819, and he was elected to the two next congresses. During his six years services in congress he was much respected by all parties, and finally succeeded in carrying through a bill for the relief of his constituents upon the Niagara frontier for the destruction of their property by the enemy in the war of 1812. He subsequently served eight years in the state senate, where he rendered very valuable services to the state, particularly as a member of the court of dernier resort. He subsequently retired from public life, and devoted his time to his private affairs and became a very wealthy man. He married Nov. 23, 1825, Harriet Foote Norton, daughter of Ebenezer Foote Norton, Esq., and Abigail Kibbe, of Canandaigua, afterwards of Buffalo, and grand-daughter of Aaron Norton and Martha Foote, of Goshen, Conn. The following is an abstract of an obituary notice of him in a Buffalo paper: "We have left for ourselves but little space in which to describe Mr. Tracy's intellectual and moral characteristics. He has of late years been chiefly distinguished among us by his extraordinary conversational talents.

He was one of the few American who cultivated this beautiful and difficult art. His mastery of it was complete, and won the admiration of all who were admitted to his society; distinguishing him while yet a youth in the circles of society in Washington. Every subject, whether gay or severe, seemed equally agreeable to him, and was treated with a wealth of diction, a felicity of expression, and a justness of thought, which can seldom be surpassed. His mind was both analitical and discursive; skeptical, yet eminently open to conviction. Always ready to abandon old opinions when he discovered that they were false, he stubbornly resisted every opinion, however venerable or common, which could not stand the tests of reason. In his youth, without instruction, he acquired sufficient knowledge of Latin to read the best known Roman authors. He had also some acquaintance with French, and was familiar with most of the philosophic and a few of the lighter writers of that language. These acquisitions he greatly prized, and was accustomed to say that they were an invaluable treasure to him. His knowledge of English literature, judged from any point, must be said to have been very extensive. He was an industrious and unprejudiced reader of the new as well as the old. He did not commit the folly of stolidly rejecting romance but found constant pleasure in the pages of Fielding, Dickins, Thackery and Bulwer. He sought eagerly for the latest publications, and was an admirer of Macauley, Tennyson, Ruskin, Longfellow and Carlyle. A lack of imagination measurably impaired his judgment upon belles-lettres, but notwithstanding this defect, his criticisms were highly valued and eagerly sought after by some of the most distinguished and successful of our own writers. It was in political and metaphysical science that his mind found its most congenial nutriment. Upon these subjects he had read much and thought more. No one who knew him and observed his keen instinct after truth, his quickness in perceiving error, the agility and subtlety of his intellect, and his judicial skepticism and fairness, can doubt that he might easily have taken high rank as a political or metaphysical writer." "Mr. Tracy's moral character was equally worthy of admiration. He has dwelt among us for more than forty years, but has done no act of which he or we need to feel ashamed. Simple in his tastes, frugal in expenditure, generous in hospitality, free to the approach of the humble, ever at hand to console or sustain the unfortunate and the distressed, ever ready to rebuke the adventurous and oversanguine; to his debtors most lenient, to his creditors paying every demand; the guide of the young, the counselor of the widowed and the orphan; an honorable foe, a faithful friend, scrupulous in the performance of every public and every private duty; he has exhibited to us for our emulation a noble example of a good citizen, wise statesman, a republican gentleman, and a kind and most liberal man." Albert H. Tracy died Sept. 12, 1859, at Buffalo, where his widow was living in 1863. They had two children: Albert Haller, born Oct. 29, 1834, graduated at Yale in 1854, was a lawyer, living at Buffalo in 1863, unmarried; Francis Walsingham, born June 9, 1839, married Sept. 25, 1862, Mary Robinson, daughter of Alanson Robinson and Zillah Townsend.

Francis, born April 13, 1797, at Norwich, and died April 23, 1802.

Harriet Frances, born Sept. 1788, at Norwich. She was the early friend of Mrs. Sigourney, whose gifted pen has done justice to her memory. She died April 25, 1830, at Norwich, unmarried.

Col. Elisha Tracy, born at Norwich, Conn., May 27, 1766, third son of Dr. Elisha Tracy, of Norwich, by his second wife, Elizabeth Dorr, was a great grand-son of Margaret Post, of the third generation. He married Oct. 31, 1796, Lucy Coit Huntington, born March 15, 1778, at Norwich, only daughter of Judge Andrew Huntington, of Norwich, by his second wife, Mrs. Hannah Phelps, of Stonington, and grand-daughter of Major Gen. Jabez Huntington and Elizabeth Backus, his first wife. [This Major Gen. Jabez Huntington, born Aug. 7, 1719, graduated at Yale in 1741, married first, Elizabeth Backus, who died in 1745, second, Hannah Williams, daughter of Rev. Ebenezer Williams and Penelope Chester, of Pomfret; son of Joshua Huntington and Hannah Perkins, and grand-son of Deacon Simon Huntington, the second, and Lydia Gager, of Norwich.] Col. Elisha Tracy was a lawyer, and they settled at Norwich, where he was frequently a member of the legislature, and a very successful lawyer, and was also a justice of the peace and a colonel of militia. He died March 10, 1842, at Norwich, where she died May 9, 1846. Their children were: William Swan, born Feb. 4, 1799, at Norwich, married Sept. 18, 1833, Mary G. Rogers, settled at Painesville, O., had three children: Elisha, a lawyer at New York in 1859; William Rogers; Mary.

Winslow, born Jan. 13, 1801, at Norwich, died May 11, 1823, unmarried. Elisha Dorr, born June 4, 1810, at Norwich, died June 12, 1823. Stephen Decatur, born July 14, 1812, at Norwich, drowned June 25, 1817. Elisha Winslow, born April 8, 1823, at Norwich, graduated at Harvard in 1843, was a lawyer, living at Chicago in 1858. Elizabeth Dorr, born July 22, 1803, at Norwich, married Oct. 29, 1829, Erastus Williams, settled at Norwich, where she died in 1855. Lucy Huntington, born May 11, 1806, at Norwich, married Sept. 11, 1833, Albert Smith, of Norwich. Hannah Phelps, born April 13, 1808, at Norwich, died May 10, 1810. Mary Griswold, born May 1, 1816, at Norwich, died Sept. 15, 1835, unmarried. Charlotte Isabella, born Sept. 30, 1819, at Norwich, married May 17, 1841, Giles M. Eaton, who died, she was living at Norwich in 1860.

Irene Burnham, born at Norwich, Conn., Nov. 18, 1744, eldest daughter of Daniel Burnham and Irene Tracy, was a great grand-daughter of Margaret Post, of the third generation. She married Nov. 2, 1763, Aaron Bushnell, born June 16, 1743, at Norwich, third son of Nathan Bushnell and Margery Jackson, of Norwich; grand-son of Nathan Bushnell and Anne Carey, of Norwich. [This Nathan Bushnell, born Feb. 12, 1686, at Norwich, married first, Dec. 2, 1713, Anne Carey, second, Sept. 12, 1715, Mehetable Allyn: youngest son of Joseph Bushnell and

Mary Leffingwell, of Norwich. That Joseph Bushnell, born May, 1651, at Saybrook, married Nov. 28, 1673, Mary Leffingwell, the eldest son of Richard Bushnell and Mary Marvin, of Saybrook. His wife, Mary Leffingwell, born Dec. 10, 1654, at Saybrook, youngest daughter of Lieut. Thomas Leffingwell, one of the original proprietors of Norwich, and Mary, his wife.] Aaron Bushnell and wife settled at Norwich, where they had six children recorded to them: Asa, born July 27, 1764, at Norwich; Joshua, born Dec. 7, 1766, at Norwich, died Jan. 13, 1767; second Joshua, born Feb. 27, 1775, at Norwich; Abigail, born Nov. 24, 1767, at Norwich; Margery, born Aug. 18, 1770, at Norwich; Mary, born Dec. 11, 1772, at Norwich.

Thomas Huntington, born at Norwich, Conn., Oct. 28, 1757, second son of Christopher Huntington and Sarah Bingham, of Norwich, was a great grand-son of Margaret Post, of the third generation. He married Oct. 14, 1779, Abigail Backus, born Nov. 6, 1761, at Norwich, youngest daughter of Ebenezer Backus, Esq., by his third wife, Sarah Clark. She died March 6, 1781, s. p. He then married ——— Griswold, and settled at Bozrah, and removed to Middletown, Vt., and removed to Dresden, N. Y., about 1820. He was a justice of the peace and deacon of the Baptist church at Middletown. His children by her were: Backus, born at Bozrah; John, born at Bozrah; Erastus, born at Bozrah; Noel, born at Middletown, Vt.; Abigail, born at Bozrah; Minerva, born at Bozrah.

APPENDIX.

The Hyde genealogy, from which the greater part of my book is copied, published by Chancellor Reuben H. Walworth, is a work of great value in the line of family history; embodying a vast amount of pedigree, and displaying clearness of perception and skill in arrangement as well as unwearied perseverance and accuracy in research. It forms a grand memorial record of paternity and lineage, spreading far and wide, but taking the nine miles square of Norwich as the center from which it radiates. Such a work is a monument to perpetuate the name of the author, Reuben H. Walworth, L. L. D., more lasting than statues of marble or pillars of granite. (Extract from Miss Calkin's work on Norwich, Conn.)

HOME OF THE TRACY'S.

The home of the Tracy's in England is Tewksbury, a borough of England, situated ten miles north-east of Gloucester, on the Avon, at its junction with the Severn, and connected with the Birmingham and Gloucestershire railway by a branch three miles in length. It has a magnificent (Abbey) church, town-hall and many public buildings. Market houses, various chapels, penitentiary, jail, literary and scientific mechanic institutes, grammar school, alms-houses, and very many charitable institutions. It has many manufactories, especially of bobinet lace, stockings, leather, nails, etc. It returns two members to the house of commons. The great battle of Tewksbury was fought immediately south of the town, from this was called "Bloody Meadow." Tewksbury is pronounced Tuksbury.

URIAH TRACY.

Uriah Tracy, of Litchfield, born at Norwich in 1755, was United States Senator from 1796 until his death. He died in Washington, July 19, 1807, and was a descendant of Winslow Tracy, the youngest son of the first John, who was Lieut. Thomas Tracy's first son, and was the first person buried in the Congressional cemetery. He was a very brilliant man, celebrated for his wit and humor.

DR. ELISHA TRACY.

Dr. Elisha Tracy graduated at Yale college in 1738, and studied for his profession with the senior Dr. Rogers. He was eminently skillful in medicine and surgery and one of the earliest advocates of inoculation as a preventive of the small-pox. He died May 1, 1783, aged 71.

PHILEMON TRACY.

Philemon Tracy, son of Dr. Elisha Tracy, was 55 years in the practice of medicine. He was able and faithful in his vocation and respected in the community. He was distinguished for his skill in the treatment of chronic diseases, discriminating, thorough and attentive in all his professional duties. He died April 26, 1837, aged 80.

FREDERICK PALMER TRACY.

Frederick Palmer Tracy made a careful examination of the records of Gloucestershire, when in England, which proved the royal descent of Thomas Tracy, of Norwich, Conn. Frederick Palmer Tracy, of Lowville, Lewis county, N. Y., died Oct. 10, aged 45. He was the son of Cyrus and Hannah Tracy, and was born at Windham, Conn., Feb. 22, 1815. He was of the seventh generation from Thomas Tracy, the first, the ancestor of all the Tracy's of Connecticut. Frederick Palmer Tracy in 1832, when a little more than 17 years of age, joined the Methodist Episcopal church, of Bozrah, Conn., and soon began to preach. In 1833, he was received on probation in the New England Conference of that denomination, and appointed to Lyme, Conn., and in 1834, to Hebron, Conn. In 1835, he was ordained a deacon and appointed to Southbridge, Mass., and in 1836, to South Boston. In 1837 he was ordained an elder, being then the youngest man known in New England to have attained that position, and was stationed at Newberg, Mass., and in 1838 at South Lyme. While at the latter place he proposed to emigrate to Oregon, and published for about a year, a monthly periodical, devoted to the extension of the idea of emigration to that almost unknown country. In 1839 he energetically pursued his favorite idea, but the plan failing, he removed in 1840, to Concord, N. H., and established a paper called "The People's Advocate." In 1842 he removed to Cambridgeport, Mass., and in 1844 to Williamsburg, Mass., where he had charge of the Methodist Episcopal church until May, 1846, when his health and voice failing he was obliged to abandon the pulpit. He visited Europe that year for the benefit of his health, returning in 1848. The succeeding summer and autumn he edited the "Cuyaga New Era," published at Auburn, N. Y., and in the spring of 1849, removed to California. He was admitted to the bar in 1851, and commenced the practice of the law in San Francisco, and was very successful. At one time he held the office of county attorney for civil business for San Francisco. He was a delegate to Chicago to the republican convention in 1860, and remained in the Atlantic States delivering political addresses in support of the nominees of the convention till his death. His remains were brought to Lyme, Conn., and his funeral took place Oct. 15, from the church where he had been a distinguished pastor. His father had died at that place a few weeks previous. Frederick Palmer Tracy left a widow and several children, when last heard from were at San Francisco. He was a man of fine parts, a clear, strong logical thinker, and an eloquent and effective speaker. While at Williamsburg he was appointed a resident member of the New England Historical and Genealogical Society, and after he removed to California he became corresponding member.

Mrs. Matilda Ormond Abbey.

Mrs. Matilda Ormond Abbey, the compiler of this book, was born in Philadelphia, daughter of Tracy Taylor, of that city, and grand-daughter of Mary Tracy, of Norwich, Conn. She was married in her native city by Rev. Benjamin Griffiths to Harvey Birchard, of Milwaukee, to which city she removed. She has one son, Harvey L. Birchard, now 28 years old. After Mr. Birchard's death, she married Col. D. C. Abbey. The Tracy's, Hyde's and Birchard's have so intermarried they seem like one family. The immediate ancestors of Harvey Birchard, of Milwaukee, lived at Wilton, then moved to Ridgeburg, Conn. His grand-father was Lieut. Isaiah Birchard, who married Sarah Betts in 1757. Harvey Birchard's brothers and sisters were: Eleia, married Mary Demming; Pheobe, married John Foster; Mirilda, married Eliazer Taylor; Lyman, died aged 22 years: Anise, married Harvey De Forrest; Stephen, married Betsey Gray; Alanson, married Esther Rockwell. Mr. Francis Birchard, nephew of Harvey Birchard, is the son of Alanson Birchard, has lived in Milwaukee many years. Elizabeth, married Charles De Forrest. Jeremiah Birchard's brother was a very rich and eccentric man, and died a bachelor. Harvey Birchard's mother was Elizabeth Abbot, she was a beautiful woman and of noble character.

Benjamin F. Tracy.

The State of New York has the honor of being the birth-place and home of many of the Tracys. The following was kindly sent me by Mr. Kelby, librarian of the Historical Society of New York, (regarding the family of the Hon. Gen. Benjamin F. Tracy, our present Secretary of the Navy.) Copied from the Historical Gazetter of Tioga county, N. Y., town of Owego. Thomas Tracy came to this vicinity with his wife and infant son, Benjamin Tracy, and settled near the mouth of Tracy creek, Broome county, in 1790. This creek receives its name from Mr. Tracy. In 1801 he removed with his family to the Holland Purchase near Buffalo. His son, Benjamin, several years afterwards returned and settled on the Apalachin creek where he raised a large family of children, one of whom is Gen. Benjamin F. Tracy, born at Owego, April 26, 1830, now a resident of Brooklyn, N. Y. Benjamin Tracy, the son of Thomas and father of our Secretary of the Navy, was born in 1795 and died in 1883. See Benjamin F. Tracy is distinguished not only for his eminent career as a lawyer but as a learned, impartial and laborious judge, and acute independent minded legislator who follows the leadership of his own judgment, subordinated to partisan interest only so far as it enhances the interests of all his constituency; a determined enemy to all political quackery. He is also distinguished as a soldier, inspired by a self-sacrificing patriotism. As a fearless able prosecuting officer of government who discharged difficult and responsible duties with clean hands and honest heart in times when speculations and stupendous frauds were nearly overwhelming it, when strong defiant rings and unscrupulous juntas were by the unstinted use of money corrupting the very sources of justice. Benjamin F. Tracy was born at Owego, N. Y., April 26, 1830. His father, Benjamin Tracy, was one of the oldest and most highly respected residents not only of Owego but of the county of Tioga. A pioneer of the southern tier, one of that band most of whom are now banished from earth whose virtue, integrity, enterprise and industry made the desert bloom and laid the foundation for wealth and culture of that beautiful region. The secret of Benjamin F. Tracy's success and his control of the popular mind may be found in his sincerity, constancy and directness. There is no deceit in his nature, men are never left in doubt about his views, and what is better he is never in doubt about himself. One always knows where to find him. His sympathy is always with the masses. No man better understands the impulses of the people than he, and he has an intense sense of justice between man and man, estimating men according to their worth. He never stands an assumed dignity nor by word or manner indicating any assumed personal superiority in his official positions. His policy was never timid or vacillating; whatever the responsibility he never hesitated to assume it but always moved promptly to the front. Perhaps nowhere in his whole career were these features more conspicuously exhibited than when discharging the duties of United States District Attorney for the eastern district of New York. In the spring of 1862 still remembered as a period of alarm to the friends of the Union cause, new levies were imperative for the Federal army, and Gov. Morgan at once appointed a committee in each senatorial district to organize a general recruiting effort. Tracy was one of the committee for Broome, Tioga and Tomkins counties. He accepted the charge and in addition to general service as a member, he received a commission from the governor, and personally recruited two regiments, the 109th and the 137th, making his headquarters at Binghampton. The active work was completed in 30 days, and Tracy was appointed colonel of the 109th with which he reported to Gen. Wool at Baltimore, in whose department it remained until transferred to that of Washington. In the spring of 1864 the regiment was ordered to join the 9th (Burnside) corps, then a part of Grant's advance. Col. Tracy led his regiment with great gallantry in the battle of the Wilderness when its loss on Friday, May 6, was upward of eighty killed and wounded. Near the close of the fighting on that day he fell exhausted and was carried from the field, urged by the staff of his commanding officer to go to the hospital. He refused, but resumed the lead of his regiment and held it through three days of the hard fighting at Spottsylvania where he completely broke down and was compelled to surrender the command to the Lieut. Colonel. When he became satisfied that months must elapse before he could again join the army, and not liking military service in a hospital he tendered his resignation and came north to recruit his health. In the following September without solicitation on his part Sec. Stanton tendered him the appointment of colonel of

127 United States colored troops which he accepted; subsequently was ordered to the command of the military post at Elmira, including the prison camp and the draft rendezvous for Western New York. This was a large and important command in the prison camp. There were at this time 10,000 prisoners. In his domestic relations Sec. Tracy is fortunate and happy. In 1850 he was united by marriage to Miss Delinda E. Catlin, a sister of Gen. Isaac S. Catlin, Ex-District Attorney of the county of Kings and one of the ablest members of the bar. Judge Tracy has three children—two daughters and a son. After retiring from the bench in 1882 as he could not resist his love for the profession he decided to resume it again. Accordingly he formed a co-partnership with William C. Dewitt, Esq., and his son, F. B. Tracy, and opened an office in Brooklyn. This was an advantageous and fortunate business relation, combining a strength, a variety of talent, learning and influence which gives it high rank in the profession, and is justly appreciated at home and abroad. Unfortunately for Judge Tracy his devotion to his judicial labors and duties impaired his health to such an extent that he was incapacitated for business, but a total abnegation from business, judicious medical treatment and a tour to Europe has nearly restored his health, and he is once more in the discharge of those duties his noble nature loves so well, and by which he has gained the high honors he so well merits and enjoys.

The Birchard's.

Thomas Birchard, aged 40, embarked for New England in a vessel called the "True Love," Sept. 20, 1635, with his wife, Mary, and six children, one of them a son, named John, aged seven years, the others were daughters. He is subsequently found at Saybrook, and was deputy from that township to the general court in 1650-51. After that there seems no record except an account of a very extensive land sale in 1656, to William

Pratt, of Martha's Vineyard, wherein he quits claim for himself in behalf of his son, John Birchard. It has been proved that this son John was one of the ten inhabitants of Norwich, Conn., accepted as freeman, and was deputy to the general court in Oct., 1691. The marriage of John Birchard and Christian Andrews, July 22, 1653, and ranging from 1654 to 1680, the birth of 14 children is recorded in Norwich, Conn. The first five children and one of later birth died in infancy. The mother was called away while her family were still young. Mr. Birchard married for his second wife, Jane, widow of Samuel Hyde, and daughter of Thomas Lee. In the settlement of Lebanon, Mr. Birchard took a prominent interest. He was one of the four original proprietors of the nine-mile tract, Norwich, purchased from the Indian chief Owaneco, in 1692. He assisted in the expense of laying out the lands and moving thither with his family in 1698, and died Nov. 17, 1702. His wife, Mrs. Jane Birchard, died at Lebanon, Jan. 21, 1723. Mr. Birchard had six sons that lived to maturity. These sons all left families. The two daughters of John Birchard, of the nine-mile tract, married John Caulkins and Jonathan Hartshorn.

Ezra Birchard, born at Norwich, Conn , Sept. 11, 1731, eldest son of John Birchard and Jane Hyde, of Norwich, was a grand-son of Thomas Hyde, of the third generation. He married Oct. 17, 1756, Martha Barret. They settled at Norwich, where they had six children recorded to them: Andrew, born April 22, 1759, at Norwich, died at Norwich, Feb. 16, 1767 ; Asahel, born June 14, 1762, at Norwich, married Jan. 1, 1788, Elizabeth Fox, at Bozrah, and settled at Lima, N. Y.; Ezra, born Aug. 9, 1766, at Norwich; second Andrew, born Dec. 2, 1768, at Norwich; Eli, born Aug. 7, 1772, at Norwich; Eunice, born Dec. 6, 1774, at Norwich.

John Birchard, born at Norwich, Conn., Sept. 30, 1733, second son of John Birchard and Jane Hyde, of Norwich, was a grand-son of Thomas Hyde, of the third generation. He married July 5, 1759, Anne Barker, and settled at Norwich, where they had three children recorded to them: Jonathan, born Nov. 11, 1763, at Norwich; Jabez, born May 16, 1765, at Norwich, married Jan. 31, 1799, Mary Downer, at Bozrah: Anne, born Dec. 4, 1761, at Norwich.

Gideon Birchard, born at Norwich, May 23, 1735, third son of John Birchard and Jane Hyde of Norwich, was a grand-son of Thomas Hyde, of the third generation. He married April 13, 1757, Eunice Abel, born March 1, 1737, second daughter of Capt. Joseph Abel, of Norwich, Conn., by his first wife, Jerusha Frink. They settled at Norwich. He died at Utica, N. Y. Their children were: Elisha, born June 14, 1758, at Norwich; Roger, born May 5, 1762, at Norwich, died Oct. 15, 1782; Jedediah, born Aug. 17, 1765, at Norwich; Gurdon, born Dec. 29, 1767, at Norwich; Erastus, born April 7, 1769; Eunice, born April 27, 1780, married her father's second cousin, Thomas Langrel Thomas, second son of Ebenezer Thomas and Deborah Hyde, of Norwich, Conn.

Phinehas Birchard, born at Norwich, Conn., Sept. 26, 1738, fourth son of John Birchard and Jane Hyde, of Norwich, was a grand-son of Thomas Hyde, of the third generation. He married June 14, 1764, Lydia Farnham, and settled at Norwich, where they had one child recorded to them: Amasa, born Jan. 19, 1765, at Norwich.

Lois Birchard, born as Norwich, Conn., Nov. 15, 1744, fourth daughter of John Birchard and Jane Hyde, of Norwich, was a grand-daughter of Thomas Hyde, of the third generation. She married May 23, 1767, Joseph Chapman, born Sept. 8, 1729, son of Joseph Chapman and Elizabeth Ames. They settled at Norwich, where she died March, 1769. His child by her was: Joseph, born Oct. 13, 1768, at Norwich. He then married in 1769, Elizabeth Abel, born Dec. 5, 1749, third daughter of Capt. Joshua Abel, by his second wife, Anna Backus.

Of the many illustrious persons who are connected with the Birchard family, one of the most noted is the Hon. Rutherford

Hayes, Ex-President of the United States. The Hayes' family can boast of a long line of honorable ancestors, which can be traced back as far as 1280, when the Hayes' and Rutherford's were two scottish chieftains, fighting side by side with Baliol, William Wallace and Robert Bruce. Both families were numbered among the nobility, owning extensive estates and having a large number of followers. The first who came to America was George Hayes, he left Scotland in 1680. He made his home in Connecticut, all that can be learned of him is that he settled in Windsor, Conn. He had one son, named George, who remained in Windsor during his life. Daniel Hayes, the son of the latter, married Sarah Lee, he lived after his marriage and until his death, at Sinisbury, Conn. Ezekiel Hayes, son of Daniel, born in 1724, was extensively engaged in manufacturing iron, especially scythes, at Bradford, Conn. Rutherford Hayes, son of Ezekiel, and grand-father of Gen. Hayes, was born at New Haven, Aug 1756. During his life-time Vermont was the eldorado of New England, and a large number of people from Connecticut, emigrated to that state, including Rutherford Hayes, who purchased a farm and established a hotel at Brattleboro'. It was at Brattleboro', the father of Gen. Hayes was born. He married Sept, 1813, Sophia Birchard, of Wilmington, Vt., whose family also emigrated from Connecticut, they having been among the wealthiest and best families of Norwich, Conn. Her ancestry by the male side can be followed in an unbroken line back to 1635, when John Birchard came to Norwich, and became one of the original proprietors of that place. Both of her grandfathers were valient soldiers of the revolution. The father of Gen. Hayes was one of those interesting characters whose life illustrates the perseverance and varied talents of our early New England people. He was a leader among his young companions in all their plays and games. He established a store at Brattleboro'. In this mercantile occupation, which he conducted on the strictest principal of honesty, he made a large number of acquaintances, who invariably became warm friends. He was a sincere christian and was a liberal and active member of his church. It was at church that he met Sophia Birchard. Too much can not be said of this admirable woman. She was a most fit companion for Rutherford Hayes, and her disposition had a most happy effect on his. He was often inclined to be silent and sad; she was gay, witty and sparkling as a mountain spring; with him, religious services were a solemn duty; with her, they were a happy privilege; she was playful, witty, light-hearted and unconsciously forced him to merriment. He was charitable and generous out of a sense of duty; she performed kind acts because she loved to make others happy. Their lives ran parallel; his keen sense of duty and her unbounded love always brought them to the same conclusion. What motive could have induced Rutherford Hayes to abandon his old home and thriving business, many warm friends. He had secured enough in business to be independent and comfortable, and yet Rutherford Hayes followed a destiny he could not fathom, and moved by an impulse none could explain, determined to set his face towards Ohio, that terrible wilderness, then the home of wild beasts and savage men, where he arrived after many difficulties, accompanied by his wife, Sophia, his two young children, Fanny and Lorenzo, and Sardes Birchard, Mrs. Hayes' brother. The years 1821-22 were terrible years for the people of Ohio. During these years a malignant fever swept over the state like a simoon, smiting with deadly blow the young and the old, in many instances, whole households were exterminated at one swoop. Rutherford Hayes was one of its victims. It was but a few short hours after the first feverish flashes ran through his limbs before the poison had performed its dreadful mission, and Rutherford Hayes passed away from this life; he died July 22, 1822, and the desolation surrounding his lovely wife can be imagined only by those who have experienced such a bereavment under similiar circumstances. Oct. 4, 1822, less than three months after the death of his father, and in his house, built four years before, was born, the Hon. Rutherford Birchard Hayes.

Unique Letter Written in 1639.

This unique and interesting letter of the Rev. John Davenport, communicated by the Rev. John Wadington, of London, was published for the first time by the Historical and Genealogical Society of New England. The Rev. John Davenport held a correspondence with Lady Mary De Vere, who was a daughter of Sir John Tracy, Kt., of Toddington, Gloucestershire, who was of the family of the Tracy's of Norwich, Conn. In the British Museum, are several letters by him, written to her from London, Rotterdam and New Haven. In the history and geneaology of the Davenport family, A. B. Davenport, Esq., has printed many of these letters entire, and from others made extracts; we quote from an account of Lady De Vere, prefixed to these letters. "Lady Mary De Vere was the wife of Horatio Lord De Vere, Baron of Tilbury, son of John De Vere, the fifteenth Earl of Oxford. During the reign of Charles, the first, he went into Holland as a commander of a regiment, sent to join with the United Princes, of Germany. He is characterized by Fuller in his "Worthies," as of excellent temper, being true of him as what is said of the Caspian Sea, "that it doth never ebb or flow;" observing a constant tenor, he is neither elated with success nor depressed by defeat. He died May 2, 1635, and was intered near his brother, Sir Francis De Vere, in Westminister Abbey. By his wife, Lady Mary De Vere, he had five daughters, his co-heirs, viz.: Elizabeth, married John Hollis, second Earl of Clare; Mary, married Sir Roger Townsend, Baronet of Raynham, in the county of Norfolk, after whose decease she married Mildmay Fane, second Earl of Westmoreland; Catherine, married first, Oliver, son and heir of Sir John St. John, of Lydiard Tregeze, second, John Lord Paulet; Anne, married the celebrated parliamentarian, Gen. Sir Thomas Lord Fairfax; Dorothy, married John Wolstenholm, Esq., eldest son of Sir John Wolstenholm, Baronet of Nostel, county York."

The Letter.

To the Right Honorable Lady Mary Vere—Madam: "By the good hand of our God, upon us my deare child is safely arrived with sundry desirable friends, as Mr. Fenwick and his lady, Mr. Whitfield, and to our great comfort thyre passage was so ordered as it appears that prayers were accepted, for they had no sickness in ye ship except a little sea-sickness; not one dead, but they brought to shore one more than was known to be in the vessel at their coming forth, for a woman was safely delivered of a child, and both are alive and well. They attained to the Haven, where they would be in seven weeks. There provisions at sea held good to ye last, about the time when we guessed they might approach near us, we sett a day apart for public extraordinary humiliation, by fasting and prayer, in which we commended them unto ye hands of our God, whom windes and seaes obey, and shortly after sent out a pinnis to pilott them to our harbour; for it was ye first ship that ever cast anchor in this place. But our pilott having watched for them a fort-night, grew weary and returned home, and the very next night, the ship came in, guided by God's hand to our towne. The sight of ye harbour did so please the captain of the ship and all the passengers that he called it Fair Haven, since that, another ship hath brought sundry passengers, and a third is expected daily, and which is more, the Lord our God hath bestowed upon us, the greatest outward privilages under the sun, to have and enjoy all His ordinances, purely dispensed in a church, gathered and constituted according to His owne mind in all things, and hath promised that in every place where he shall sett his name, He will come unto his people and bless them, and now madam my desire is that your La-P (lady-ship) may be assured that whatever interest I have in J X, and by him in fellowship with his people at the throne of grace, it is wholly for your advantage, if in anything I may express ye reality of my thankfulness to your honour, for my favours formerly received, and for your helpfulness to my little one in carrying him in your coach to Sir Theodore Maherne, for advice about his neck, and for your cost in a coate, of which bounty and labour of your love, my servant, Ann, hath made full report to us. The Lord recompense ye, same to your La-P, and to your noble family, one-hundred-fold, I hope befor this time He hath rebuked the feverness and smallpox in your family, which has lately affected it, and will make the losse of Mr. St. Jo, a mercy to your daughter, whom I love and honor in the Lord. The Lord ye holy one of Israil, our redeemer, hath undertaken to teach his people to profitt as well by his provedences as by his ordinances even by all his dispensations; accordingly I believe He will, and pray that he may be pleased gratiously to make this losse be her gain, and these trials evidances of his fatherly love, both to your La-P, and her, that mortality of earthly comforts and the dissolubleness of the marriage-bond, with ye creature may quicken us to secure our interest in the everlasting God, and our marriage with the Lord J. C., by an everlasting covenant of his grace, which nothing can dissolve. My wife presenteth her humble service with much thankfulness to your La-P. We both desire in like manner to salute my Lady Wake, and all your noble daughters. Had I time, I would write to Mrs. Watson, your scribe, at present, I have no more liberty than to salute her, and to let her know that if her affections stand hetherward, I shall be gladly be useful to her in what I may and do think that it would be comfortable to her many wais. But it is God who setts the bounds of our habitations, to whose everlasting doings I commend your Lady-ship with all yours in Jesus Christ, in whom I rest. Your honorable La-P, much obliged in ye Lord."

JOHN DAVENPORT.

Quinnepiack, 28 vf e 7 month, 1639.

The Fashions of Norwich

The fashions of Norwich in 1757. The dress of that middle period can not be eulogized for its simplicity, or economy. The wardrobe of the higher circle, was rich and extravagant, and among the females of all classes, there was a passion for gathering and having articles of attire, beyond what was necessary for present use, or even years ahead. It was an object of ambition to have a chest full of linen, a pillow bier of stockings, and other articles in proportion laid by. In this connection we present a schedule of the wardrobe of widow "Elizabeth White," of Norwich, as contained in the inventory of her effects, taken Aug. 16, 1757. She was a daughter of Samuel Bliss, and relict of Daniel White, of Middletown. After the death of her husband in 1726, she returned to Norwich, and died there July 2, 1757, aged 71. The items of jewelry, plate and apparel, were circumstantially enumerated, but we give them in abridged form : she had many gowns of durog striped stuff, plaid stuff, black-silk crape, and blue camlet, a scarlet cloth cloak, and one of blue satin, flowered mantel and fur below scarf, a woolen petticoat with border, camlet riding-hood, long silk hood, velvet hood, white hoods brimed with laces and ribbons, a silk bonnet, and 19 dress caps, cambric lace handkerchiefs, silk and 16 linen ones, a lace apron embroidered, one green taffety, and 14 aprons in all, a silver girdle, a blue girdle, four pieces of flowered satin, many yards of silver ribbon, a parcel of crewels, and handsome fans, Turkey worked chairs, a gold jewel necklace, deaths-head, gold ring, set of gold sleeve buttons, plain gold ring, gold locket, silver hair-pin, silver cloak-clasps, a precious stone, set in silver, for a button, a large silver tankard, a silver cup with two handles, one silver cup with one handle, silver spoons. The next generation was still more extravagant. Richer goods were imported, and more splendor was exhibited. The following is an illustrative instance : The daughters of Gen. Jabez Huntington were sent successively, at the ages of 14 and 15 to finish their education at a boarding school in Boston. The lady who kept the establishment was of high social standing, and made it a point, of taking her pupils often in society, that their manners might be formed according to the prevailing codes of politeness and etiquette. Of course the wardrobe prepared for the young ladies was rich in articles of ornament and display. One of the daughters, who had been carefully fitted out with twelve elegant silk dresses, had been but a short time in Boston, when her instructress wrote to her parents, requesting that another dress should be procured for her, made of a certain rich fabric, that had recently been imported, in order that her appearance in society might be equal to her rank. A thirteenth robe of silk of the requisite richness was sent. Before the revolution, wigs full and curled for clergyman and other dignitaries were white, and powdered, red cloaks, or rouquelaurs, and buckles or bows of ribbon at the knees and in the shoes, were worn by gentlemen. Even young boys were often arrayed in cocked hats, small clothes and knee buckles. If on ceremonious occasions, wigs were not worn, gentlemen had their hair crimped, curled and powdered by barbers. A full dress for gentlemen were mostly made of silk, with trimmings of gold and silver lace. The waist-coat most always highly embroidered. Ladies wore trains to their dresses or gowns, often quite long, and when they walked out they threw the end over the right arm. They dressed their feet in silk stockings, sharp-toed slippers, always made of rich material, mostly of embroidered satin, and with very high heels. At one time sharply gored gowns, and cumberous hoops were the fashion. Cushions stuffed with wool, covered with silk, were used to dress the hair. At one period, feathers were much worn on the head, surmounting a high turban of gauze. Parasols were unknown, or of rare occurance, but a fan, nearly a foot and a half in length, was often carried open to keep off the sun. A lady in full dress for great occasions, displayed a rich brocade, with open skirt and trail, front skirt trimmed and embroidered elegantly, with stomacher and full ruffles of real lace at the elbows. As the great struggle for liberty gradually over-shadowed the land, and the sacrifices necessary to consummate the revolution, began to be appreciated, a decided change took place in regard to dress, amusements, and display; women discarded all imported articles, ornaments, etc., arrayed themselves wholly in domestic goods. Gentlemen also, who had been accustomed to appear in society in the daintiest costume, following the example set by the women, discarded their shining stocks, their linen cambric ruffies, silk stockings, silver buckles, and other articles of foreign production, and went back to leather shoe-strings, home-spun clothes, etc.

Copied from "Picturesque Canada," Page 87.

A handsome new church was dedicated in 1876 to La Bonne Sainte Anne de Beaupre. To it were removed the old altar and pulpit, both of the seventeenth century, and the relics and original ornaments of the old church. Among these, are an altar-piece by Le Brun, the gift of the Marquis de Tracy; a silver reliquary, and a painting by Le Francois, both the gift of Mons. Le Laval; a chasubel, worked by Anne of Austria, and a bone from the finger of Sainte Anne.

A great number of the Norwich Tracy's have been graduates of Yale college.

Letter of SIR BERNARD BURKE, C. B., L. L. D., Ulster King of Arms, Dublin Castle. Author of the Extinct and Dormant Peerages; The Landed Gentry; The General Armory; Vicissitudes of Families, and Reminiscences Ancestral, Anecdotal and Historic.

DUBLIN CASTLE, IRELAND, November 3, 1888.

DEAR MRS. ABBEY:

I am and have been so ill since I last wrote to you, that I am obliged to use the pen of an amanuensis. I do not like waiting until I am better and able with my own hand to express how much I am pleased with your admirable history of the GREAT HOUSE OF TRACY. I have CAREFULLY gone through the volume and my estimate is formed on a minute perusal. When I return to my usual pursuits, which, please God, will be soon, I trust to obtain some genealogical additions for your acceptance.

With esteem and regard, yours most truly,

J. BERNARD BURKE, Ulster.

www.ingramcontent.com/pod-product-compliance
Lightning Source LLC
Chambersburg PA
CBHW030353170426
43202CB00010B/1360